The Inner Champion

A Seven-Week Practical Guide
to
Peace, Happiness and Miracles

Kathleen Quinlan MSW

Cover design Lily Domishev | www.ldormishev.com
From an original drawing by Allison Reese

Table of Contents

WEEK TWO -
CREATING YOUR PERSONAL EXPERIENCE

WEEK THREE -
ACCEPTING YOUR CREATIVE AUTHORITY

WEEK FOUR -
ALLOWING LOVE TO TRANSFORM YOUR LIFE

WEEK FIVE -
TAKING BACK YOUR TRUE IDENTITY

WEEK SIX -
THE CHALLENGE OF CONSCIOUS CREATION

WEEK SEVEN -
FULFILLING YOUR DREAMS for YOUR LIFE
and YOUR WORLD

Introduction

I have written this book to help you experience the peace and safety that await each of us, when we discover our relationship with the inner self. This is the eternal, unlimited self we are before we come into the physical world. It is our true self, created by the reality of Love that flows through all living things. Our very essence is the pure creative power of Love. Although we can never be separated from what we are, the intense demands of our daily lives often block us from knowing this great self is within us. We struggle, believing that our limited, physical self is all that we are. It is the responsibility of the inner self to awaken us to our power and to the peace and safety that are our birthright. I call this self the Inner Champion because of its role as our advocate. Rising to our aid when we feel powerless and unaware of its magnificent presence, it uses its immense power to clear a path for our conscious return home to Love and for the fulfillment of our dreams.

The inner self became our Champion the instant we suddenly wondered what it would be like to be completely different from our true self. What would it feel like to be the opposite of our joyous, unlimited selves? Much like children who dress up pretending to be someone else, we simply wanted to expand our knowledge of ourselves. We decided to step away from our inner self, for just a moment. But unlike playful children, our desire carried indescribable imaginative power, and at our command, a terrifying new world emerged from the innocent wish to know ourselves as the reverse of who we are!

This is what happened when we were born in this world. Still conscious of our inner self, we felt an irresistible desire to be something else. We split away from our inner, non-physical reality, and came into the physical world, in the words of the poet Wordsworth, 'trailing clouds of glory...' But with each passing day, the memory of the joyous creativity, the deep peace and the security of the Love we knew began to fade. Cut off from the inner self we felt utterly alone, with no consciousness that what seemed to be happening *to us* was the result of *our choice*. What was supposed to be an innocent, imaginative exercise, suddenly became a terrifying experience, as we stepped away from our loving reality and our limitless freedom into a world of deepest limitation, fear and chaos.

The inner self knows that we cannot change the reality of Love. But we still have the absolute freedom to create an imaginative, *personal* experience of a world that is the opposite of Love in every way. It sees the fear and chaos we experience in the physical world and knows it is a nightmare we need to be awakened from. As our Champion, it will prove to us that the madness we have created is the result of our limitless imaginative freedom. It reflects the choice we made to experience ourselves and our world without the reality of Love. Although we made a terrible mistake that has brought us incredible suffering, we still have the freedom now to make another choice. We can return to the consciousness of our loving reality and the Inner Champion is determined to help us make this choice.

In order to do this, it must make us aware of its presence within us. As we learn to trust its guidance, it will undo the distorted beliefs about our deserving that block the acceptance of Love. Although we lost the conscious awareness of the inner self with our birth in the physical world, we are still immersed in its greater reality and our connection to its immense power continues to create our experience.

This book is designed to help you recognize the presence of your inner self and understand how its energy creates your experience in the physical world. To reverse the belief in powerlessness and regain your creative freedom, you need to learn how your own distorted beliefs about self-worth and empowerment become an unconscious program for the constant creation of difficulties in your life. These ideas form the basis of your experience, very much like the data in a computer program. The energy of the inner self then flows through this program, constantly creating your life according to the expectations that come from the core beliefs you developed about yourself and your world.

In the physical world, the search for Love becomes the foundation for the structure of our beliefs. Although it is beyond our conscious awareness, when we are born we are still deeply connected to the knowledge that the reality of Love is the source of our peace and safety. It is part of our eternal connection to the inner self and stays with us, even in the darkness and profound confusion of our experience in the physical world.

Since we lost the memory of who and what we are when we split away from our inner self, we had to make a new self-concept based on the need for the Love we lost, knowing intuitively it is the *only* source of peace and safety. Searching for Love to survive and make sense out of the madness of this world, we used our experience in early relationships as the basis for understanding ourselves and the nature of our new 'reality.' Given our complete dependence on parents and other caregivers in our early life, we accepted their judgements about our worth and did not doubt their validity. We relied on them to show us the meaning of Love and our deserving to be loved. The joyous certainty of our true worth was replaced by a new self-concept based on the evaluation of others whose acceptance we desperately needed.

In order for us to reunite with the inner self and our power, we must learn that the concept of ourselves we created is not who we are. It grew out of our original decision to split away from the inner self, and we are *still adapting to* the devastating personal reality that came from that decision.

The Inner Champion is determined to show us that the tyranny we experience because of that error was *never intended* to be a permanent existence for us. It came from an innocent desire for a brief adventure, and no imaginary experience of ourselves as powerless in a world of fear and madness will ever be a substitute for the magnificence that we are and the joyous fulfillment that is our birthright.

Although we may rail against the experience that comes from our distorted beliefs for a very long time, we do have the knowledge within us that our suffering violates our right to happiness and creative freedom. This realization will rise again within us as we face personal crises that shatter old beliefs about ourselves and our world that no longer serve us. When we despair because the limitations of our personal histories leave us without any answers, we can finally go within and let the Inner Champion show us those limitations do not exist.

As we open to this awareness, and learn to cooperate with the inner self, it will intervene to deepen our awareness of its presence. Its goal is to encompass more and more of our personality and our physical experience, replacing the distortions we have accepted about ourselves with the recognition of our unalterable deserving to be loved and to be loving. As this healing occurs, the acceptance of our worth will restore the creative authority we need to transform our lives and consciously begin our journey home.

You have the right to awaken to the true power that comes from your relationship with the Inner Champion. You also have the responsibility to let this awakening happen for you. Now more than ever it is essential for us to reclaim the limitless creative freedom that is natural for us when we align ourselves with our inner self. It is increasingly evident in our lives and in our world that we are facing complex problems that have no viable solutions we can draw upon from the limitations of our ordinary experience. The Inner Champion will help us let go of beliefs that tell us we are powerless to change what clearly violates our right to peace and safety and show us the reality of Love and its power.

How To Use This Book

The guide that follows reflects the model for healing I've developed in my work with people experiencing a wide range of physical, psychological and emotional difficulties. I have discovered that regardless of the presenting problem, teaching the individual about the reality of the inner self and its loving power is the beginning of the healing process.

Throughout the book I use the terms 'spiritual,' 'inner' or 'true' self to describe the loving source within each of us. I have worked with people from many different religious affiliations and cultural backgrounds and I have found that these terms are readily accepted when they are understood to refer to the greater loving reality from which all life springs. However, these names should be considered interchangeable for whatever names you associate with an eternal loving source, such as God, Goddess, Yahweh, All That Is, your Guardian Angel and other descriptors for the infinite reality of Love.

The daily segments that follow are arranged to help you awaken more each day to your relationship with the inner self. The meditations at the end of each lesson are brief but, in spite of their brevity, they are effective tools for progressively deeper and more enjoyable experiences with your own Inner Champion.

Whether you are currently in the midst of a personal crisis, or simply realize you deserve much greater fulfillment in your life, this guide can help you begin the transformation you desire.

A Seven-Week Practical Guide

to

Peace, Happiness and Miracles

WEEK ONE - RECLAIMING YOUR BIRTHRIGHT to LOVE

Day 1. Discovering Your Inner Self - the Champion Within You

My hope is to inspire and challenge you each day to discover the reality of your inner self. When you strip away all the layers of the physical self, what's left is your true or inner Self. It is the real self that we are when we release all of the judgment and fear we accumulate throughout our lives and accept the self-worth that restores our birthright to Love. Because the inner self is determined to help us reclaim this legacy, it is truly our Inner Champion.

This self is the powerful loving source of your life. It is not separate from you, but a living breathing presence within you. The awareness of this self *is* within you. We can never extinguish the spark within us that assures us of our reality. We are spiritual beings, but when we immerse ourselves in the physical world and struggle with its limitations, we can become so distracted by the chaos and complexity in our lives, that we lose our awareness of this wonderful and powerful resource.

Our relationship with the inner self is the foundation of our experience. Each day you'll be given ideas about the nature of this partnership and a brief meditation to help you discover your own relationship with this self. With its support, you can set new goals for your life with greater confidence that it is your Champion and will help you achieve these goals. You may not have met this self yet, but these daily exercises will help you become intimately acquainted with this part of you. You can learn to trust this self and call on it to free you from the past and bring you the peace and happiness you deserve.

With this first meditation, you can begin to experience a true partnership with your inner self, one that will bring greater fulfillment than you ever dreamed was possible for you. You can refuse to accept the loneliness and victimization that comes from feeling apart from your inner self, and consciously choose to experience the reality of Love. Aligned once again with Love, the Inner Champion will begin to manifest this Love in your life and in your world, to help create the peace and safety it sorely needs. This is its task and its power.

Your desire is *everything* here. Your inner self loves you beyond all imagining and because of this great Love it is determined to show you the creative freedom you're destined to experience. As you open your heart and ask to feel

1

the reality of this self, it will eagerly show you its loving presence, and encourage you to trust its guidance more and more each day.

As you begin your journey with this first meditation, you're invited to turn away from whatever problems you may be facing in your daily life and step back into the peace of your relationship with the inner self and remember your birthright to Love.

Meditation

For the first meditation, sit quietly, breathe slowly and easily and let yourself gently relax. With your eyes closed, see yourself standing alone in front of a beautiful red curtain on a large stage. Imagine that you see your life and your world pictured before you as a great drama. Turn now and go back behind the curtain. See your inner self standing before you with open arms. Let yourself be encircled in this loving embrace for a few moments. Then open your eyes and carry this Love into your day.

Day 2. The Power of Your Intention

Yesterday I described the importance of your desire in helping you experience the reality of the inner self. I said that your desire is *everything*, and this is not an exaggeration. Most of us don't think of our intention alone as powerful. When we want something, we assume we'll have to work very hard to get it. However, as you begin to realize the limitlessness of Love, you'll be able to understand your birthright to the creative freedom it brings. Because of this, the inner self is constantly reading our desires and bringing about the results we truly want.

This doesn't mean you don't need to do anything to create what you want, but the burden for *how* it's created is *not* the job of your physical self. The outcome is created at a spiritual level and is manifested for you at the physical level according to your desire, your imagination and your expectations. This includes all of the inspiration and resources necessary to produce the desired outcome.

We've all seen dramatic evidence of this process in emergencies where spontaneous, superhuman strength is demonstrated by an otherwise frail person. For example, when a ninety-pound grandmother wants to lift up a truck to release a grandchild pinned under it the inner self responds to her intention immediately and floods her physical body with the adrenalin she needs to lift it.

All of our experience is created this way, as the inner self responds to our desires.

In this situation the grandmother's intention manifested immediately. Because it was an emergency and required immediate action, all potentially interfering beliefs were thrown aside for that moment. She did not stop to consider whether or not she *deserved* this strength, or if it were too difficult to accomplish what she wanted. This opened a clear channel for her inner self to deliver what she needed. Whatever self-doubts or unworthiness she had vanished in the instant her need for physical strength became her only desire. And the response from her inner self was immediate and powerful.

If we don't get what we believe we want, it's always because some deeper, often unconscious desire is in place within us, confounding our conscious intent. The inner self always responds to our deepest desire. When you don't get what you've asked for, you can be sure some competing belief has blocked the inner self's ability to deliver what you consciously say you want.

The usual culprit thwarting the outcome is some form of feeling 'not deserving.' To enjoy your creative freedom, you need to let the inner self heal whatever feelings of 'not deserving' are blocking it.

Meditation

As you start the day, gently close your eyes and let yourself relax. See your inner self appear before you and reach into your heart, pulling out the old thorns hidden deeply within it. Know that you are worthy of everything. Let yourself sink into the joy of your innocence. Open your eyes and set your intention to carry this feeling with you throughout the day.

Day 3. Healing the Blocks to Love

We are deeply and completely loved. The goal of the inner self is to bring us the peace, happiness and miracles love holds for us. To do this, it must heal the old, distorted beliefs that block our willingness to accept it.

Since the search for love is such a powerful motivation, you might wonder why we would ever refuse it. It is not that we consciously turn our backs on love; it is the unconscious feeling of 'not deserving' that keeps us from accepting love.

When we are born our first task is to find the love we intuitively know we need. We immediately look to parents and others who care for us to show us the meaning of love and that we deserve to be loved. Unfortunately, many of us experience love as conditional or abusive. Because it is too frightening to think there is something wrong with the adults we depend on, we think there is something wrong with *us*. We decide we are not good enough to be loved and this becomes part of an unconscious pattern of belief about ourselves that we repeat over and over.

Unlike the peace and happiness that come with accepting love, struggle, suffering and guilt are the natural consequence of feeling undeserving of love. They are such common experiences for most of us, that we accept them as a natural part of reality, like gravity.

It is easy to see why we do not believe that peace, happiness and miracles are our natural state of being. We need a gentle re-education by the inner self to learn this is true. The inner self knows that regardless of our feelings of unworthiness, nothing we have ever done can alter the truth that we are worthy and deserve to be loved.

An angel is an entity with wings, who defies everything mankind believes in. We too have wings, but they vanish when we rely on what we have learned in our physical experience. One of the keys to getting them back is to use the *defiance* of an angel. Defy what you've learned about the realities of struggle, suffering and guilt and let the inner self teach you the reality of Love.

Meditation

As you start your day, sit quietly with your eyes closed and let yourself relax. Imagine yourself in a beautiful place in nature at your favorite time of day. Ask the inner self to fill you with the love that brings you the peace, happiness and miracles you truly deserve. Let yourself rest in this love for a few moments. Open your eyes and ask the inner self to help you remember this peace throughout your day.

Day 4. Your Spiritual Rights: The Foundation of Healing

Most of us don't associate healing with our rights, but our spiritual rights are the *foundation* of healing. They are the heritage of the limitless Love that created us, and they are the same rights outlined in the U.S. Declaration of Independence.

"We hold these truths to be self-evident that all men are created equal, that they are endowed by their Creator with certain unalienable rights, that among these are Life, Liberty and the pursuit of Happiness."

This is not just eloquent language. It's a powerful statement about the rights we are guaranteed in our relationship with our Creator.

Notice the language in the Declaration of Independence describes our rights by stating 'that *among* these are...' That is, there are other rights that are also self-evident and unalienable. These are rights that we must also have in order to fulfill our fundamental guarantees: the right to peace, the right to prosperity, the right to love and to be loved and the right to power. The awareness of our rights is something that each of us has deep within us. We are born with it and we cannot lose it, but we forget about it because we're immersed in the severe limitations of physical experience. We forget about the reality of the inner self and its desire to restore these rights, which are meant to transform our lives.

It is essential for us to remember these rights and learn to believe deeply in their reality, because our beliefs are the template for our physical experience.

We have a structure within us that's very much like the old floppy discs which were used to save data on our computers. It sits between our physical experience and the inner self. From the moment we're born everything we experience including the emotions that were part of those experiences, gets stored in it. This is not symbolic input. It is literal, just like the data saved on a computer.

As we grow up, we use our experiences to create beliefs in major areas of our lives. These are dimensions of experience that we all share: the meaning of love, our deserving to be loved and to be loving, our sense of self-worth, our power and our rights to peace and safety.

Because we have the creative freedom to construct our personal realities, our beliefs in these areas become an unconscious template or pattern that the inner self must use to produce our experience. Many of us, because of early painful experiences have distorted ideas in each of these areas and deep feelings of unworthiness. We believe we do not deserve to be loved, we are not powerful and the world is a frightening place where we cannot experience peace and safety.

These beliefs, although they were reasonable conclusions as we grew up, *now* rob us of our unalienable rights. They prevent our Inner Champion, from bringing us the happiness we were born to have in our lives, and they need to be healed.

This healing will occur as you deepen your relationship with the Inner Champion. Its purpose is to transform distorted beliefs about your unworthiness and replace them with the truth that you are worthy of *everything*. This restores the peace, happiness and miracles that are your birthright.

Meditation

Find a comfortable position and gently close your eyes. Let yourself take several relaxing breaths and, as you exhale, imagine that you are releasing old beliefs that no longer serve you. Then listen to the inner self tell you that you are indeed worthy of everything and you are safe. It is the limitless Love within you that guarantees your safety and your peace. Then open your eyes and carry this knowingness into your day.

Day 5. Forgiveness: The Key to Your Spiritual Heritage

Yesterday I talked about our spiritual rights to peace, to prosperity, to be loved and to be loving, to power and to freedom. This is the natural endowment of our loving creation and we may expect practical and powerful changes in our lives because of this legacy. It's a new vision of our future in this world as we grow to embrace our spiritual heritage.

We can never be completely separated from this knowledge, but it's often forgotten because of the pain and struggle of our physical experience. We were created as immaculate reflections of Love, and this innocence is our essence and the source of our power. Yet most of us grow up with experiences that result in deeply held beliefs in our unworthiness, and we're left feeling that we do not deserve the peace and happiness we were born to enjoy.

The inner self sees these beliefs as errors we have developed about who and what we are. It knows we cannot change our eternal innocence. True forgiveness, as it is used by the Inner Champion, is the spiritual transformation of these ideas, because they block the grace that should flow easily into our lives, bringing us our spiritual heritage.

Seen in this light, forgiveness is essential for spiritual growth and fulfillment. In this process, the Inner Champion changes past pain into the loving energy that is our true nature, but we are responsible for cooperating with this process. We can do this by becoming conscious of our spiritual rights, and particularly of our deserving to be loved and to be loving.

Although we've always had this knowledge deep within us, as we become conscious of our rights, our egos will try to persuade us such freedom is preposterous. Because the ego embodies our experiences of limitation and all of our beliefs in our bondage, this part of us will rail against the reality of our freedom.

You'll need patience and compassion for yourself as you grow and move through this process of discovery and learn new ways of looking at yourself and your life. Our spiritual heritage is the opposite of what most of us have learned to expect in this world. And although these concepts may feel unfamiliar at first, we were born with this knowledge and have a right to reconnect with it.

The inner self knows who we are and what we deserve. It isn't swayed by the clamor of our egos. It asks for a tiny willingness from us at this stage of our growth to open us to the healing it has been striving to give us. It is our Champion. Its job is to release us from the pain that prevents us from receiving peace and happiness and bring about the positive changes this heritage is meant to bring to us.

Meditation

Relax for a moment with your eyes closed. Breathe in deeply and with a sharp exhale, and imagine yourself forcefully releasing all your fears, your doubts about your worth and all other questions. Then look up and open yourself to receive the flood of golden white light that comes forth from the Inner Champion into all that you are. Open your eyes and remember that this light is *always* with you.

Day 6. Forgiveness and the Championship of the Inner Self

The inner self is your Champion. Because we are deeply and completely loved, its job as our Champion is to correct beliefs that are barriers to love and block our spiritual rights to peace, happiness and miracles. This is the meaning of Forgiveness.

Your inner self is the core of what you are, without the distortions created by your personal history. In its Championship on your behalf, it holds the knowledge of your rights, which you left behind on your journey into the physical world. It constantly reassures you of your spiritual identity, awakening you to this reality by helping you remember your rights and the happiness you were born to have.

The inner self uses physical experience as a constant feedback mechanism to show us the difference between what we have in this world and the peace and happiness that we still deeply know is our birthright.

The crises we all experience at different times in our lives accelerate this recognition. When we finally feel exhausted from years of struggle against limitation and opposition and when all the old external sources of support fail us, we are reaching that time in our growth when we are ready to turn within and be guided home by the inner self.

When you suffer from depression, anxiety and other emotional problems, as you know, it can feel as if there is no way out of suffering. You can feel imprisoned by your feelings and powerless to find the emotional and psychological stability you deserve.

This is where your understanding and belief in your spiritual rights become so essential in developing new tools for healing and growth, including the acceptance of professional help for additional support when you feel the need for greater assistance. Knowing that you truly have these rights can help you learn to seek and accept the help of others who can support your growth, as you learn new ways to feel strong and capable in your day-to-day experience.

As you become more aware that peace is your birthright, you gradually realize that it is your natural state of being. It is *not* natural to believe you are at the mercy of feelings or situations that are disturbing. Yet many of us accept that this is a natural part of being human, given the chaos that we perceive in our lives and in our world.

As you learn to listen to your inner self and to feel and accept its loving championship, you will begin to realize that anything that disturbs your peace is *not* natural. It is actually a violation of your right to peace and happiness. It calls for the corrective action of the Inner Champion to heal whatever disturbs you and restore your peace.

The promise of peace as an unalienable human right given to us in our creation is total. As incomprehensible as this may be to our physical selves, this means the experience of peace in *all* of our personal reality, including our community, our country and our world.

The inner self longs to give you the peace you desire so deeply, but you must be willing to accept it, knowing that you fully deserve the love its championship will bring.

Meditation

With your eyes closed, gently relax and imagine yourself resting in a quiet place in nature. See your inner self appear and take your hands, walking you down a path that leads to a beautiful tall mirror. Look into the mirror and see yourself serving your highest potential of Light. Feel the peace and happiness of this state of being. Open your eyes and carry this image with you into your day.

Day 7. The Role of Your Emotions

Your inner self is determined to restore your spiritual rights to peace, prosperity, love, power and freedom. These rights are inseparable from who and what you truly are. They are endowments meant to insure the happiness guaranteed in your creation.

Awakening to the reality of your spiritual rights can help you see the areas of your life where your rights are clearly being violated. This awareness helps you cooperate with the inner self as it uses the energy of forgiveness to free you from feeling undeserving, and the consequences it brings to your life.

There are many ways to join with your inner self to accelerate your spiritual growth. One of the most powerful is to learn the role of your emotions in liberating you from the past and strengthening the consciousness of your creative authority in the present.

Our emotions give us vital feedback about our experience. They come from our perceptions about what we are experiencing and give us the information we need to make choices about how to respond. They are meant to be identified and explored and then expressed in a balanced manner.

However, very early in our lives we learn to shape our emotional reactions according to what we believe will be accepted by parents and others whose love we crave. As children, when we try to express the natural range of our feelings, we're often met with parental disapproval. Most adults fear the expression of strong emotions, especially anger. Because of this, many of us were raised to show only approved emotions, and we learned to suppress much of what we truly felt in order to get the love and affirmation we needed.

But suppressing our feelings doesn't mean they have vanished. They continue to exist as powerful energy within us, contained in the memory and belief structure that determines how our personal reality is created.

As we grow up, if we experience rejection, victimization, violence and other painful events, this structure will be full of powerful, unexpressed feelings. The weight of these emotions, sometimes suppressed for decades, can result in depression, anxiety and other emotional symptoms as well as physical problems.

These emotional burdens keep us tied to the past and unable to realize our spiritual rights and our power in the present. Since our emotions are important channels of communication between the spiritual and the physical selves, suppressing our feelings also weakens this connection. When these channels are open, you can experience your connection with the inner self as a source of loving support and guidance.

Since we have the right to peace and happiness, we are also given the means to exercise these rights by releasing old emotional patterns. This release is a completely natural process and can be learned with patience, commitment and the powerful assistance of your inner self. Throughout this book we offer several approaches you can use to enhance your emotional freedom.

Meditation

Sit comfortably with your eyes closed. Open the soles of your feet and allow the loving energies of mother earth to flow upward into your physical body, keeping you strong and renewing your determination to be a vehicle for this Love in your life and in your world. Open your eyes and take this spiritual stamina into your day.

WEEK TWO -
CREATING YOUR PERSONAL EXPERIENCE

Day 8. Guilt and the Birth of Your Negative Ego

The inner self is your core self. It is the loving, powerful identity that is uniquely you, all worthy and magnificent in spite of the limited and difficult experiences you may have in the physical world that tell you otherwise. It knows who and what you are.

Its job is to bring you back to the realization of your identity so that you can experience the peace and happiness you are meant to enjoy. To do this, it uses forgiveness to free you from the beliefs in unworthiness you have accumulated throughout your life and clear the way for you to finally accept being loved.

Our emotions are important tools on this journey. They can keep us connected to our personal power and to the fulfillment of our goals. They help us evaluate our experience, giving us important feedback about what we need to change to reach those goals. They also keep us connected to the compassionate guidance of the inner self. However, most of us learn early in our lives to deny strong feelings, especially our anger; and it is the denial of this emotion that quickly causes problems that have far reaching effects on our mental and physical health and spiritual growth.

When we first feel the rise of anger as a child, we are not afraid of it. We know instinctively that it is our natural reaction to frustration, feeling victimized or in some way denied the love we desperately need. But when parents and others disapprove of or discipline us for expressing anger, we not only decide that our anger is unacceptable, we also conclude that we have done something wrong. Or we conclude that there is something wrong with us and we begin to feel the first pangs of guilt.

This is a powerful turning point because it is the beginning of our perceived loss of innocence and the development of our distortions about love and our deserving to receive it. We need the love of those who are caring for us and so we must believe in their infallibility. At least early in our development, we are not going to question their judgment.

Over time, fearing this judgment and believing more in our guilt, we increasingly deny our natural anger and automatically substitute it with guilt. It's not that our anger is completely buried, but because of this early conditioning, we repress it, which now has a powerful effect on our self-concept and on our lives.

The reason for this is that guilt is not a true emotion. In order for a feeling to be valid, it must have both positive and negative polarities. But guilt is *always* negative. It creates a strong belief in our unworthiness, hides the awareness of our innocence, and confirms our perception that we are separate from the inner self.

The inner self brings us back to the awareness of innocence that is the core of our spiritual identity. It is *only* the belief in our unworthiness that blocks this awareness. The inner self looks past the distortions about our worth knowing they come from our personal histories. They are errors that block the truth about who and what we are and they need to be healed. For the inner self, this is the meaning of forgiveness.

By holding onto guilt, we arrogantly substitute our unworthy self-concept for the innocence of our creation. We shun forgiveness and the love it offers by telling the inner self, "I hear what you're saying about my worth, but I know better. I know what I've done and I'm so guilty, even you don't have the power to heal me!" However, we can't be held hostage to the past. We are free beings and can choose to end guilt. To do this we need to welcome forgiveness. We have to want peace, happiness and miracles more than we want to suffer to prove we are right, that our guilt is more powerful than the inner self's power to heal it.

Meditation

Today, find your comfortable position and, with your eyes closed, breathe gently and slowly. Know that the distorted ideas you now hold about yourself come from beliefs you have developed from your personal experience. But this is *not* who you are. Feel the presence of your inner self. Imagine it opening the top of your head and pulling out the old, false images you have carried. Now see it take a tiny vial of golden white liquid and pour it gently into your mind, filling your mind with the truth of who you are. Let yourself feel the confidence of this new identity. Open your eyes and greet your day with this new assurance.

Day 9. Your Beliefs: The Template for Experience

Our physical experience is the energy of our personal histories, coalesced into physical form. We make decisions about who we are and what we can expect in our lives based on the beliefs we develop in our early experiences. Then, these beliefs become the foundation of our personal reality. They are stored in an energetic structure between the inner self and our physical self. The great, creative energy of the inner self flows continuously through this structure, manifesting our bodies and our lives, according to the desire, imagination and expectation it contains.

If you could open up the top of your head, lift out your belief structure and look at it the way a physician examines an X-ray, you would instantly see the source of your experience in this life, with all of its richness and challenges.

It might help to imagine this structure as having dimension or an energetic thickness. The side you can see shows your personal history translated into the major categories of beliefs we all share: the nature of love, your deserving to be loved and to be loving, your self-worth, your power and your rights to peace and safety. These beliefs are usually well formed by the time you are five to seven years old. They become an unconscious template the inner self uses to create your personal reality. If you were able to read the substance of each of these categories of belief, you would see that your current life is reflecting your expectations in each of these areas.

Then imagine your inner self looking at the *other* side of this structure. It sees the clusters of discrete events, now held as memories, which are producing all of your limited beliefs. It sees the painful experiences that you have had. They constrict the flow of spiritual energy that is meant to bring you happiness by creating negative emotions that reinforce your distorted beliefs. In place of a luminous opening for It to flood your life with joy, the inner self sees a largely darkened space, riddled with the energy constrictions of powerful negative emotions.

The inner self's use of forgiveness clears this structure for you so the beliefs you hold reflect the truth of your worth. Through this pure space its energy can spring into your life bringing you peace, happiness and miracles and dissolving blockages created by your past experiences.

As you cooperate and partner with this clearing, you'll gradually experience greater peace in your life and in your world. However, you need to let the structure between your spiritual reality and your physical experience become an immaculate pathway for the materialization of forgiveness.

There are many ways to cooperate with this process. Learning to honor your feelings and releasing those that no longer serve you will help you cooperate with this healing.

The Forgiveness Meditation is an excellent resource for this purpose. It is a beautiful and powerful tool to let the inner self gently help you release the past and it's available as a free download on CDbaby.com.

Meditation

Today, sit quietly and comfortably with your eyes closed. Imagine feeling weighed down by a large boulder on your torso. This stone contains years of suppressed anger that presses down on you, leaving you feeling weighed down and feeling unable to move forward. Ask the inner self to help you remove this weight from you forever. Then sense yourself lift it easily and throw it off with great determination, freeing yourself of this burden at last. Open your eyes and feel this new confidence throughout your day.

Day 10. The Memory of Your Freedom

The knowledge of our right to freedom is deep within us. When we feel mounting pressure in our lives, relationships, work or financial obligations, or when the noise of daily life seems deafening, the voice within that speaks to us of our freedom cannot be silenced.

We are spiritual, unlimited beings clothed in flesh. We come into the physical world to learn about ourselves in an experience that is the complete reversal of our unbounded, loving nature. In our innocent desire to know ourselves more fully, we chose to create an experience of limitation instead of freedom and opposition instead of oneness. Much like exuberant children who playfully put on 'scary' costumes at Halloween for the fun of a completely alternative experience, our brave decision to dream of embodiment and immerse ourselves in physical reality was intended to be a brief, exciting learning experience.

However, in order to make the experience of limitation seem real, we had to completely forget our spiritual reality. And as we dreamed and took our first step away from our oneness with the inner self into the physical world, it instantly became real for us - so real that as we took that first imaginative step, we immediately believed we were bound and had no memory of our freedom or our loving heritage.

And we are still dreaming! It's time to wake up from the nightmare we have believed was real for so long. It's time to realize we are truly free and return to the creative authority we are meant to experience.

One way to quickly get in touch with your freedom is by telling yourself the truth about those areas of your life where you feel imprisoned. Self-pity about these situations will not liberate you. It will only convince you even more that the dream is real and you are a victim. It numbs you to the presence of love and to your power.

But as you look at your life through the lens of your spiritual rights and see areas of unhappiness as clear violations of these rights, you can give voice to the anger that is meant to help free you.

Allowing yourself to acknowledge the anger and disappointment you feel at your perceived powerlessness will lead you to a deeper knowing that your victimization is not, *cannot* be your destiny. This will open you to the guidance of the inner self reminding you of the Love within that guarantees your freedom.

Meditation

Closing your eyes now, let yourself gently relax. Know that it is truly time for you to wake up from the dream and demand your birthright! See yourself climbing to the top of a mountain. Now open your mouth and bellow as if your life depended on it, "I demand my birthright to peace and safety, to prosperity, to freedom and to Love!" Let yourself feel the power of claiming your birthright at last. Breathe into this feeling of power. Open your eyes and carry this freedom into your day.

Day 11. The Experience of Love in the Physical World

We were created by Love. It fuels our bodies and our lives, and it sings behind every breath we take! If this is true, why is it so many of us feel love is elusive? Why are loving relationships seemingly so difficult to find and sustain? Why is it sometimes difficult to feel the love of the inner self?

When we're born, we step away from the reality of Love and the knowledge of our oneness with It. We temporarily forsake the reality and security of the Love we have known and we enter the physical world to learn about ourselves in a completely alien environment - a world of limitation where we believe we are separate from Love.

Imagine awakening in an utterly unfamiliar realm, with no memory of Love. It's easy to understand why the desire to find the Love we believe we've lost becomes urgent and why we desperately look to those around us to show us the meaning of Love.

In our vulnerability and innocence, we rely on the quality of our interactions with our parents and those around us to teach us what Love must be. Too often, however, our experience with our parents and others produces false ideas about the meaning of Love.

As a result, we develop beliefs about Love which are deeply distorted, but which become the unconscious pattern for the relationships in our lives. Love remains elusive, and our hearts carry the wounds of a long and painful quest!

But the inner self always holds the truth of the Love that you are. And despite your fears, it will carry you home to it again.

Meditation

Find a comfortable position and, with your eyes closed, breathe gently and let yourself begin to relax. Sense yourself surrounded from your head to your toes with a beautiful, soft blue light. Remembering what it's like to be taken care of completely, let yourself sink into the joy of feeling the Love you believed you had lost. Open your eyes and bring this joy with you into the day.

Day 12. Handling the Rise of Emotions as You Heal

Love is a mighty creative force within us. Our job is to learn to surrender to it, because it's only through our complete immersion in Love that we can truly return to our power and our true identity.

But how can we let ourselves accept this Love, when on some profound level, we have concluded from our life experiences that we don't deserve to be loved? As we become conscious of this block, we can summon the great power of our intention to signal our willingness to return to Love and begin the process of transformation.

In a sense what happens is that the inner self responds to our desire for spiritual growth by gently beginning to walk us back through the layers of distortions about Love and about the identity we have developed throughout our life.

In this process we step back from the personal self-concept we created based largely on childhood beliefs and begin a journey we deeply desire and deserve back to the maturity and joy of our oneness with inner self.

Because the personality has become so entrenched in its own self-image and beliefs and has been living in denial of powerful emotions buried throughout your life, this transformation can usher in periods of intense conflict with yourself and with others. Fear, anger and sadness may rise for release in long waves that leave you feeling confused and uncertain about what's happening to you.

Be patient with yourself in this process. Seek the support of others who care about you, seek professional guidance if you need additional help and have faith in the inexhaustible Love within you. Know you are being cleared of debris from many years of perceived separation from your true, inner self.

As you go about your day, set your intention to feel the presence of this Love as a palpable reality within you. Sense it as a beautiful light that is with you every moment and behind every breath that you take.

If you become aware of feeling fearful or angry, acknowledge these feelings. You can do this by simply saying to yourself, "Yes, I feel this fear or anger." Then turn within to your inner self and open yourself to the power of the Love that you are.

Meditation

For today, as you close your eyes and relax, allow yourself to feel the truth that your worth transcends all worldly judgment about who and what you are. Let yourself feel the changeless perfection of your worth. Be grateful that you're willing to return to the love of the inner self so that you may remember your worth once again. Open your eyes and carry this confidence into your day.

Day 13. Feeling the Limitless Power of Love Once Again

Deep within us we continue to hold the knowledge of our true identity as the creation of Love. Throughout our lives we will be given many opportunities to remember our reality and use this discovery to begin a new life of freedom in this world. When we finally become exhausted from struggling against limitations we *know* intuitively *cannot* be our destiny, we can become willing to let go of old, distorted ideas about ourselves, and allow the inner self to gently lead us back to our true identity.

That identity, your true core self is Love beyond all imagining. It is a depth of Love that is apart from anything we experience as love in this world. So when we try to imagine what this Love would feel like, we'll probably think of what we believe is ideal love on this plane and think in terms of devotion, unconditional acceptance, and security.

We probably will not think of Love as power, without limits or opposition. Yet this is the essence of Love and it is our essential nature. It is the power and creative freedom that flows from our oneness with the reality of Love.

It might help to understand the endowment of power in our creation by thinking about what we consider to be perfect parental love. That is, when you imagine loving a child totally, isn't it natural to think, "I want my child to have everything he or she wants and to be completely happy and at peace in their world?"

Why would we hold our own creator to a lower standard? We do not have the power to give our children complete freedom and happiness, but the reality of Love *does* have that power. And in its perfect and limitless love for us, we are given complete creative freedom of being and the tools to insure our desire for peace, happiness and miracles will be fulfilled.

Children intuitively know their creative freedom. And the child within you still remembers the mastery you knew in the spiritual realm, where your desires instantly appeared before your very eyes.

This is why the relationship between Cinderella and the Fairy Godmother is so universally known. The story exists in hundreds of forms in cultures around the world because it is the archetypal symbol of the relationship between the spiritual and the physical self and the love that invests the physical self with creative freedom.

We quickly forget this freedom, though, as we come into the physical world and adapt to its severe limitations. One moment we are in a dimension of exuberant freedom where our dreams are instantly manifested, and in the next, we come into physical reality and lose the mastery we knew in our spiritual home. We feel separate from the source of our being and in opposition to everything around us.

This results in our deeply held belief we must either control our environment or be controlled by it. We have lost the mastery we once knew and as a result we experience a world that seems opposed to us rather than part of us.

We can return to our freedom of being. We are responsible for doing so. We are responsible for returning to the championship of the inner self, letting it guide us to the innocence that restores our power, through the process of forgiveness.

Meditation

Today, let yourself be drawn back into Love and to the wonder of its limitless power. Close your eyes and breathe gently and deeply. Sense the inner self standing behind you, placing its hands tenderly over the top of your head. Feel the radiance of this loving power as it descends into your body and extends through your reality without opposition. Let the inner self reveal the miracle the lesson of forgiveness, perfectly learned, will bring into your life and your world.

Day 14. Using Your Present Power to Release the Past

The power and the creative freedom of Love is our natural state of being. It is always available to us in the present. We interfere with this perfectly natural state and deny our freedom and power when we chain ourselves to past ideas about who we truly are.

We use our memory like a club in our daily lives by ignoring the purity of the present moment that holds our remembrance of Love and our worth. Instead we remember only the past, where we learned we did not deserve this love.

It's like the use of plates in old-fashioned photography. In order to produce a true picture, the photographer needed to insert a fresh plate into the camera before covering his head and capturing the image he wanted. If he mistakenly used an old plate that already contained a picture, the result would be distorted.

The production of our physical experience is very similar to this process in that we actually choose in each present moment what memory we want to insert into our waking consciousness to produce the picture of reality we experience. Although this process ordinarily happens outside of our awareness and at lightning speed, *we can slow it down*. We can learn to take conscious charge of this process and exert the creative authority we once knew so well in our spiritual home. That too is a memory that's just as available to us as the memory of bondage that comes from the belief in our unworthiness.

Your creative authority is a completely natural function of what you are. That means you've already had experiences with this power. It appears at those times when your deep desire for something has momentarily cast aside your beliefs in your frailty and allows what you wanted to manifest before your very eyes.

As I suggested earlier, you can clearly see this in emergency situations when immediate strength is needed to rescue someone in danger. In these instances, the rescuer consciously demands physical power. He or she inserts a new template in the stream of spiritual energy producing his experience, and the inner self immediately stops the old production of weakness and delivers the power that is needed for the rescue.

This is an excellent example of the creative power that is always available to you. The question of deserving is completely absent from the conscious intent of the rescuer and the response of the inner self. The belief in 'not deserving' keeps you from remembering your core self, the self you are without your personal history. The urgency of the situation, and the power needed to override any judgment of worth momentarily created the perfect alignment of the physical self with the pure power of the inner self.

This is why the process of forgiveness directed by the inner self is so beautiful and powerful. Your willingness to surrender to it allows the inner self to insert the immaculate template of your real forgiven self into the creative energy stream producing the picture of your reality. It brings you the power to more consistently create the life you desire without the blockage of the past.

Meditation

Today as you close your eyes, feel yourself sinking away from the physical body and into the loving embrace of the inner self. Feel the power of the inner self and know that this is *your* power to be used more and more consciously for the creation of the life you truly desire for yourself and your world. Know that your willingness to look within is a profound step in your growth and your freedom. Open your eyes and take this empowerment into your day.

WEEK THREE - ACCEPTING YOUR CREATIVE AUTHORITY

Day 15. The Power of Becoming What You Desire

As you test the way the inner self responds to your desires for changing your life, you will quickly see that when you have an intense desire for something and focus on it briefly and with powerful resolve, you can override the unconscious obstacles that usually interfere with your conscious desires and get what you ask for.

As you experiment with your creative freedom in this way, you are learning the fundamental law of reality creation: that is, what you concentrate on becomes your experience.

To use the earlier example of the photographic plates, when you stop using old distorted plates and insert a completely blank one instead, infusing it with one desired image, you create a pure opening for the inner self to pour its energy through it, constructing your reality according to its design. You are doing exactly what Gandhi intended with his famous mandate to *'become* the change you wish to see.'

As you learn to trust the inner self and its guidance you'll want to experience the powerful results possible, when you completely let go of what you hold in your mind and consciously fill it with your desire. You can use this method of *becoming* what you want to see in order to *produce* what you want, very naturally in your own life.

Meditation

As you begin your day, set aside time to close your eyes, and gently let yourself relax. Imagine that the soles of your feet open and everything you currently believe drains out of your being. Open your heart and see and feel the image of what you want. Let the image grow within you until it expands and you feel yourself completely immersed in it. See it radiate beyond your physical self into your life and your world. Repeat the exercise in the evening if you wish, as you drift off to sleep.

Day 16. Using Playfulness to Accelerate Creative Abilities

Adopting a playful attitude toward your spiritual development is a powerful way to deepen your relationship with the inner self and accelerate the impact of this great presence in your experience.

As you grasp the power that is naturally available within you to create change in your life, it is very tempting to turn to your ego to figure out how to direct that power and to assume you need to struggle and work hard to become your true self.

Most of us have so completely accepted the belief that we have to work hard to achieve anything of value, it seems incomprehensible to suggest that hard work is actually an impediment to spiritual growth. This is because to be what we already *are* cannot take effort. As this becomes more evident we realize the only challenge any of us face as we return to our inner self, is the stunning recognition that we already *are* this self.

In practical terms this has wonderful implications for your life and your understanding of what it truly means to be responsible for your spiritual growth. It means first of all that the highest vision of yourself already exists. Your job is to accept this as true and admit that, although you don't know what this vision looks like, the inner self *does* know and will help you gradually become this vision.

Your willingness to accept the state of not knowing what this vision is creates a vacant space within you for the inner self to show you this vision and to bring you the changes you want in your life. This requires trust and a relaxed state of allowance for you to feel the impact of summoning the transformation.

The inner self wants to make you happy and it knows how to do this. So when you want something, your effort at the physical level to figure out how to make it happen actually interferes with the flawless delivery of change that occurs when you get out of the way and leave the change you want completely up to the inner self. By assuming a relaxed openness for the inner self to fill your days with happiness, you'll see that a playful, childlike expectation of fulfillment truly aligns you in a powerful way with the happiness the inner self longs to bring you.

Meditation

As you begin the day, you can use this brief visualization to help you affirm your intent to maintain this wonderful playfulness.

Close your eyes and take a few relaxing breaths. See yourself standing with the inner self behind you. In front of you is a large photographic plate, almost as tall as you are. This has all the old images you've held as your identity. Now grasp the plate with one hand and playfully toss it aside. See yourself filled with a blazing white light as the inner self floods you with the vision of your true self. Let yourself feel a childlike delight as you wonder what happiness the day will bring.

Day 17. The Desire of the Inner Self to Show You Its Love

Soon after I wrote the previous segment on the power of playfulness, my inner self surprised me with a wonderful gift and the opportunity to experience my own wisdom! I think you'll appreciate the fun and the ease of my own unexpected experience with this subject and try the experiment I discovered to let the inner self deliver more happiness to you as well.

I had ordered a book titled *E Squared* by Pam Grout, in spite of consciously telling myself I probably wouldn't enjoy it! I was put off by the subtitle; *'Nine experiments to prove your thoughts create your reality.'* "Well, really," I told myself, "I don't need to read another book like this. This is what I teach and this is a principle that guides my own life." Nevertheless, I felt drawn to read it. I hadn't even finished the first chapter before I knew I enjoyed the book and it would be a gift for me in many ways.

With the very first experiment I experienced a wonderful demonstration of the power of a playful, expectant openness to create the space for the inner self to bring more happiness into my life.

The first experiment calls for the reader to ask the inner self, what she calls the FP or 'field of potentialities,' to make its presence known by asking for a blessing or a gift within 48 hrs. This result will be a clear sign and she suggests that it will feel as if the FP (inner self) were saying "My pleasure!"

I had barely stated my intention, when a lovely event began to unfold.

I'd gone to Minneapolis months earlier and discovered a new brand of kefir. Kefir is a drinkable form of yogurt. I drink it often and this particular brand was the most delicious I had ever tasted.

When I got back home I looked for it everywhere but couldn't find it. I spoke with dairy managers, store managers and even the corporate headquarters for the brand itself, but no one could explain why it was not available where I lived. I felt discouraged because I knew I really should have been able to manifest it, no matter what the corporate barriers seemed be! My scan of the dairy aisles eventually slowed and I resigned myself to enjoying it only when I went to Minneapolis.

But soon after I started this experiment, I was running errands and made a quick stop at the grocery store. As I passed the dairy aisle, I saw two clerks dressed as pirates for Halloween; one of them was unloading a flat in front of the dairy case.

Before I knew it, I stopped and heard myself starting the old line of questions about how incomprehensible it was that the store couldn't get this kefir when they had everything else the brand makes!

The young man I was speaking to pushed his eye patch up under his pirate bandana and said earnestly, "What does it look like, Ma'am?" As if on cue, both of us looked down at the flat he was unloading. "Wellllll...," I started to say, "It looks like, it looks like THAT!!!! Oh my goodness, there it is! You've got it!" The pirate looked at me, beaming "How many would you like?" I threw my arms around him and gave him a big hug. As I danced to the check-stand with my three bottles, I heard him say to his fellow pirate, "Boy, we'd better keep *this* stuff in stock!"

Try the experiment yourself. Hold the inner self's feet to the fire! Or hold your *own* feet to the fire. Insist on an indisputable expression of the presence of the inner self and its desire for your happiness within a specified period of time.

In the coming weeks, we'll look at how to extend your success with your clearly defined intention, so that your days are filled more often with happiness and the certainty of the benevolent presence of the inner self. We'll also look at some of the common ways we can interfere with this process and how to prevent the self-sabotage of our happiness.

Meditation

Find your comfortable position and gently close your eyes. Know that the life your inner self desires for you is, in many ways, the reverse of your current experience. Its job is to bring you happiness and only happiness. Let yourself remember an event that made you indescribably happy. Let yourself feel this happiness again now. Then imagine yourself surprised today with something unexpected that fills you with happiness. Open your eyes and bring this expectation into your day.

Day 18. How to Release the Fear of Embracing Your Power

As you learn to trust the inner self and have more experience with Its eagerness to help you, you will see that playful requests, such as asking for a specific outcome within a limited time frame, can sometimes bring amazing results. And the answer may come with astonishing speed, and a sweetness that clearly shows you the desire of the inner self to make you happy.

But sometimes you may have difficulty with this kind of experiment, either because you don't feel confident you can really attribute certain events with your request or because sometimes it seems you don't get any response at all!

The different outcomes in this process reflect some of the core challenges we face as we begin to accept responsibility for the creation of our personal realities. The very decision to directly ask the inner self to show you a blessing may bring up fears about the reality of inner, spiritual experience you hadn't realized you felt.

You might find yourself thinking, "What if it doesn't work?" or "What if everyone else gets an answer to *their* demand and I don't?" "Maybe I don't even have an Inner Champion or if I do have one, maybe it's decided I don't deserve a gift or maybe It's given up on me..."

Or conversely, "What if it *does* work? What does that really mean? Doesn't it mean I really *do* create my experience? All of it? No, it can't really mean that! I'm not ready to take responsibility for all that I see..."

Sometimes we encounter these fears indirectly. You might be thrilled initially. You let yourself jump into this kind of experiment and before you know it, the heavens open up and one gift or several land at your feet. But before you have time to feel the happiness it was intended to bring you, some negative event occurs to end your pleasure.

Maybe in the midst of your excitement, someone criticizes you or calls you with bad news. Perhaps you stumble and fall or are harmed in some other way. You could allow your happiness to be reversed and express your fears, including one of the most deeply held of all fearful beliefs on this plane - that there's always a price to exact for joy.

Or you could be compassionate and patient with yourself and remember that in the transition from victimization to dominion, you're going to have one foot in one dimension and one foot in the other for a while. The fears that you experience are just the yammer of your ego, trying to insure your allegiance to it rather than to your Inner Champion.

One of the reasons this particular experiment is a valuable learning tool, is that it gives you a gentle but powerful opportunity to experience the beneficence and love of the inner self before your ego knows what's happening. Love and happiness, joy and delight - these so confound the ego's belief in chaos and suffering that before it realizes what's going on and can try to stop you, the Inner Champion embraces you and pulls you back from behind the heavy curtain of your delusions, surprising you with Its loving gift.

Even though you'll find yourself going back and forth between Love and fear for some time, once the Inner Champion has opened the curtain, allowing the Light to assert its presence in your reality, it will eventually transform what you now perceive as dark and impenetrable. No ego can withstand the force of Love.

You may want to try the experiment again. Perhaps this time, insist on the presence of your Inner Champion making itself evident not just for you - but for someone else too!

Meditation

As you find your comfortable position, close your eyes and sense the presence of your Inner Champion as a sweet warmth within your heart. Feel it become a radiance that fills your entire being, joyously supporting you behind every breath that you take. Open your eyes and feel this sweetness within you during the day.

Day 19. Defying the Ego's Claim That You Are Powerless

I hope you are starting to feel a sense of excitement and enthusiasm about your relationship with the inner self, and the creative freedom that's opening up for you.

When you summon the inner self with determination and an open heart it will gladly show you its presence. As you let yourself feel the wonder of this new way of being and consciously decide to feel grateful, accepting that you deserve to be loved in this way, you will soon find that the happy effects continue to manifest for you.

In a sense there's an infinite backlog of grace within each of us that is held back by old beliefs in suffering and limitation. As you respond to the guidance of the inner self to accept the Love that's been kept safe for you and maintain this state of receptivity, you will open yourself to receiving the flow of grace into your reality

You *can* do this. In truth, it is the most natural thing you can do because in allowing yourself to be happy, you align yourself with your *right* to happiness. To do otherwise is to fight yourself and the inner self by maintaining that you know better about who you are and what your purpose is!

You can refuse to bow to the ego's insistence that this is dangerous territory - that you do not deserve happiness, that you will misuse the power of creative freedom, and that victimization is your true nature.

Again, you cannot remind yourself too often that your spiritual awakening is the reverse of everything you've learned about the limitations of physical experience. You are here to demonstrate your birthright by allowing true happiness, peace and miracles to become the core of your experience. The world doesn't need any more demonstrations of suffering. You can help to bring the justice of Love to the world by allowing the joy of your creation to shine in your own life, and then through you to illuminate everyone and everything around you.

Ask the inner self to show you evidence of your Love extending beyond you, to your close relationships, your workplace, perhaps or your community or elsewhere in the world - as you consciously focus your Love beyond what you perceive to be yourself.

As before, be open and ready for the evidence that your heart has been touched by a gift from the inner self.

Meditation

Today, find your comfortable position and gently close your eyes. As you relax, feel your inner self place its hands softly over your eyes. Sense a delightful, tingling energy fill your eyes with the Light of true vision. Now as the inner self removes its hands, see a picture of your reality transformed through your new vision. Open your sparkling eyes and use them now to see a new day.

Day 20. Your Right to Dominion: Manifesting Miracles

We have an absolute right to dominion in our lives. Dominion is the conscious use of our creative authority to produce our personal experience according to what we truly want. This power comes naturally from our relationship with the inner self. In order to learn to trust the Love and guidance of this relationship in our lives, we need to be willing to be much more conscious of how our experience reflects the action of the inner self as it delivers what we want. Notice I said what we want, but not necessarily what we've asked for, because the inner self always gives us what we truly want. And if there's a difference between what you ask for and what you get, it's because there is a competing desire you're not conscious of that's being respected by the inner self.

The culprit is usually some sense of not deserving that blocks our ability to consistently bring forth what we ask for. Miracles are the expression of this natural function of our oneness with Love. In this sense miracles simply reflect the power that comes from the innocence of this oneness and flows naturally into our experience when it is not blocked by the beliefs in unworthiness that come from our past experiences.

We have the right to allow miracles to come into in our life and we have a responsibility to do so. The manifestation of what we term miracles simply involves the recognition that in each moment, there are an infinite range of probable versions of every experience. Miracles demonstrate this by shifting what we believe about a situation to another perception that expresses a new, desired outcome.

I'll give you a beautiful example of this allowance.

Years ago I was on an unforgettable journey in Peru with a diverse group of people from around the country. We were traveling with the author, Alberto Villoldo and a very old, sweet Brazilian shaman.

One morning we headed out in an open boat across Paracas Bay to visit one of the immense figures in the famous Nasca Lines, a candelabra etched in the desert and unchanged after thousands of years. The bay was choppy and we were shrouded in a fog so thick we could barely see one another. My heart sank as I became afraid we'd miss it entirely because of the fog.

I was sitting next to the little shaman who was calmly smoking his pipe. In my frustration, I suddenly cried out saying "Oh, I wish the sun would come out!!!" And with this, the little man stood up in the rocking boat and, while absentmindedly tamping his pipe tobacco with one hand, calmly raised his other hand to the sky. To our utter astonishment, immediately the clouds parted and the sun appeared, flooding the bay with its sunshine!

Now, this was one of many such displays of power we witnessed on this trip - the power that flows naturally from our innocence. The shaman brought forth a miracle at will because in that moment he simply swept aside any unworthiness in his personal history and allowed Love's pure power to come into his experience.

When you feel blocked in your efforts to create what you've asked for, voice your frustration, but then see this as an invitation to open yourself to deeper immersion in the Love of your inner self.

Meditation

One very beautiful and powerful way to do this is by listening to music that you deeply love. Today, preferably using headphones, close your eyes, breathe in gently and listen. Feel the inner self using this music to tell you how completely you are loved.

See what power this brings to you.

Day 21. Giving Complex Problems to Your Inner Self

As you learn to trust the inner self, you'll realize its guidance is truly within you and always available to you. The challenge is to be willing to ask for it and trust it has the power to deliver what you need.

This is a process that requires humility and faith, because when we're born, we quickly forget our relationship with the inner self and the creative freedom of this union. We step away from our true self and begin a journey of separation from that self, learning to adapt to the laws of the physical world. We identify with the ego, trusting its guidance, and believing its lie that our safety and success depend on the control and manipulation of our experience.

Eventually, the dissatisfaction and unhappiness that are common for so many of us will compel us to search for deeper meaning and the peace and happiness we intuitively sense should be ours.

Even though this begins a journey that will return you to the empowerment you once knew, it may take many seemingly miraculous experiences before you are willing to rely more consistently on your relationship with the inner self, allowing it to assist you and provide the answers you need.

And sometimes it takes the experience of intense pressure or impending failure to bring us to our knees so that we become little enough and humble enough to get 'through the eye of the needle,' accepting that we have exhausted all the solutions we thought were possible in a very difficult, complex situation.

But this is exactly what the Inner Champion waits for, because when you feel there aren't any solutions to a problem, it just means you've eliminated all the possible answers devised by your personality. But there are many other solutions available when you create the space for these answers to come by giving the problem to the Inner Champion

When you return to the full awareness of your relationship with the inner self, you'll begin to automatically sense its guidance in these circumstances and let it guide you back to your peace of mind and your creative freedom.

Until then you can learn to recognize when you need to give a situation to the inner self to resolve a dilemma or receive clear direction. When something seems complex and you feel increasingly frustrated with your inability to produce a positive outcome, know that you're being invited to give the problem to the inner self.

That's when you can learn to step aside, ask for help and expect to receive an answer. Then stay out of the way. Resist the temptation to tinker with it yourself one more time. Truly step aside and watch the peace and power that comes to you from your inner self, rather than your personality.

Meditation

Gently close your eyes and let yourself begin to relax. Sense yourself settling back into the arms of your Inner Self. As you feel the comfort of this Love, see one specific problem that is frustrating you. Release your need to find a solution today and give the problem to the Inner Self. Feel the relief and expectancy of putting it *completely* into its hands. Open your eyes and go forward in your day, allowing the inner self show you its ability to bring you the answers you need.

WEEK FOUR -
ALLOWING LOVE TO TRANSFORM YOUR LIFE

Day 22. Forgiveness: The Power of Your Innocence

The creative authority to consciously create your experience is the natural result of your birthright to the reality of Love. This power becomes more available to you as you finally allow the healing of beliefs that you are unworthy and don't deserve to be healed. This is the true meaning of forgiveness from the perspective of the inner self. It takes you gently back to the awareness of your worthiness and your perfection.

Notice I didn't say 'takes you back to the state of your perfection and worthiness'. I said back to your *awareness of this state*, because you've never left this state of worth. You've never lost your identity as it was given to you in your creation. How could you?

Think of this for a moment. Do you really believe it's possible to change your nature? This would mean you actually had the power to change the perfection of your creation by the reality of Love. What kind of power would that be, to defy the limitless power of Love? Is there such power? Do you have it?

Of course not! The answer is a resounding 'No!' No matter how much you believe you have altered your perfect self and corrupted you self into the opposite of that perfection, you didn't do it. You couldn't do it. You dreamed that you did, and that dream has terrified you for a very long time and you've suffered because of it. But that perceived nightmare was never real. It was a nightmare and that's all it has ever been. It's a nightmare you have the right and the responsibility to awaken from, and the Inner Champion through its use of forgiveness will facilitate this transformation.

The color of blue violet, an exquisite shade of purple, is often associated with forgiveness and with the power it brings when we release the limitations of mankind's belief in its essential unworthiness. Merlin's attire in the legend of King Arthur is an ancient illustration of the blue violet light and the creative power of forgiveness.

Meditation

For today's meditation, gently close your eyes and let yourself relax. See your Inner Champion standing before you, holding a beautiful blue violet robe. It will get the color just right! Turn around and let it enfold you in this magnificent cloak. The instant you feel its warmth, sense yourself filled with its power and then project this energy out through the center of your forehead as a beam of blue violet light. Project it into those areas of your life where you perceive difficulties right now and let this energy do its healing work for you. Let it show you the true power of forgiveness.

Day 23. Witnessing the Impact of Your Loving Energy

As you learn to trust the reality of your inner self and its responsiveness to your needs, it will create opportunities that show you the impact of your energy in the physical world and give you greater confidence in its reality and your ability to consciously direct it.

Here's a wonderful example of an experience in my life which was designed to show me the reality and unmistakable impact of my own energy.

Years ago I attended a conference on alternative medicine sponsored by the World Health Organization. I came with my friend Jill, who was to meet a renowned Chinese practitioner of QiGong, an ancient energetic healing technique. Jill's doctoral advisor had seen a demonstration by this master, Dr. Huang Rui Sheng, while traveling in China. Even though she wasn't formally aware of Jill's interest in healing, she said that while watching the demonstration, she immediately felt she should get his address and give it to her.

Jill, herself a gifted healer, was very interested in QiGong and decided to write him to ask if he accepted students. He wrote back immediately and said that her timing was perfect - that he was coming to the US for the first time for a conference and would meet with her then.

We arrived late and by the time we got to the ballroom, thousands of people were already seated. As we stood in the back and tried to see an empty seat, I saw a man in the middle of the room stand up and turn toward the back of the room wildly waving his arms.

Now, we were very far from this man, but we were the only people standing in the back of this immense room. So, as improbable as it seemed, I wondered if this could be the presenter who was expecting to meet Jill.

I tugged on her sleeve and started down the center aisle toward this man, whom I now could see was grinning and clearly motioning to us!

When we got to his aisle, he eagerly gestured for us to join him, showing us an empty seat on either side of where he was sitting. He was Chinese and didn't speak any English, however he was with another Chinese man, who spoke English and introduced himself as Dr. Ming Fang. He told us this was indeed Master Tan Rui Sheng, the presenter, and that his friend was happy to meet us.

Master Tan Rui Sheng was a slight man, with joyous, child-like energy who looked much younger than his 60 years. He gestured for us to sit on either side of him, took out a pad and eagerly sketched a figure showing us the meridians used in QiGong healing.

We watched, fascinated, as he enthusiastically drew instructions for this ancient technique. The three of us were completely absorbed with this and weren't listening as the conference chair stepped up to the podium. After a few opening remarks, I finally heard the end of his comments as he said it gave him great pleasure to introduce the featured presenter, Master Tan Rui Sheng, who was here to introduce this form of QiGong for the first time in the United States!

I was very surprised! I didn't realize he was the featured presenter and I had no idea his presentation was so historically significant.

Still drawing for Jill and not understanding English, he didn't know he was being introduced until Dr. Fang got up and tapped him on the shoulder, pointing to the stage!

With that, Master Tan Rui Sheng nodded, got up, bowed slightly to Jill and to me and quickly made his way up to the stage.

He was to demonstrate the technique on a woman who was unable to walk and was scheduled for knee replacements. She was wheeled out onto the stage and lifted up to lie on an exam table. Master Tan Rui Sheng then took a position about twenty feet from her and began the slow, precise QiGong movements that change the patient's energy to create the needed healing.

As he began to do the poses, I was filled with a sense of compassion for this sweet man, as he began this important demonstration in front of several thousand people. I decided to send him my own loving energy and closed my eyes briefly, imagining an arched beam of golden white light going from my heart to him, immersing him in the light.

The audience watched in amazement as he gave a beautiful demonstration of this ancient Chinese technique. When he was finished, the woman was helped down from the table and walked off the stage without any assistance! The audience jumped to their feet and gave him a standing ovation. After bowing to their applause, he ran back up the side aisle, smiling, shaking his head, and gesturing with his hands as if saying "stop", while he seemed to be looking at me!

And to my amazement, he continued with this display as he got back and stood in front of me! Mystified, I looked at Dr. Fang for an explanation. He smiled and said, "Master says thank you for your beautiful energy, but please do not send it to me while I'm focused in this way! It's very powerful and it distracted me!"

In retrospect, I realize this entire sequence of events was an amazing gift from my inner self. It came at a time when I deeply wanted confirmation of its existence and my own ability to summon its loving power at will.

It is your right to have demonstrations like this to strengthen your recognition of your creative abilities. Open yourself to the presence of the inner self and to your own authority. Ask for the evidence of its Love, as you want and need it each day. It is constantly available to you. When you feel fearful or confused about something, know you're being given an opportunity to seek help within.

Meditation

Today close your eyes and let yourself relax. See yourself walking along a path in a majestic forest. Marveling at its beauty, you hear the sound of a waterfall and, turning sharply, you see it just ahead of you. Hear the voice of your inner self asking you to step into this glistening shower. As you feel its warmth and purity, know that it is washing away your self-doubt and fear of failure – filling you with strength and confidence. Open your eyes and carry this certainty into your day.

Day 24. Expanding Your Set Point for Happiness

As you feel your heart open to the unfolding of your dreams, it's essential to remember the powerful role of deserving in the manifestation of what you truly want.

Each of us has what you might think of as a set point for our deserving. That is, as we grow up we decide how much love, happiness, wealth, peace and so on we can have in our lives. This is a very specific determination. It's a decision formed early in our lives that creates definite, allowable levels in each area of well-being and then becomes the unconscious barriers that block us when we try to go beyond them.

I described this earlier when I suggested that sometimes just as you start enjoying a sustained period of happiness, and feel confident it's going to last, something adverse happens. It seems to come out of nowhere and detracts from that happiness or reverses it altogether.

This simply means you've gone beyond your set point for happiness and there'll be an automatic adjustment that brings you back down to the level of happiness dictated by your own gauge in this area. These are personal set points that come from your early experience and beliefs. And these barriers become even more powerful when you accept deeply held worldly beliefs that happiness isn't possible for us in this world and our efforts to find true happiness will be punished.

The belief that we must pay a price for joy is so ingrained in our human experience, we don't recognize it as a belief. Instead, we see it as part of our reality, like gravity, and therefore impossible to change.

This helps explain why you may become anxious when everything starts going well in your life, because both your own beliefs and the mass consciousness tell you that this is not normal and unhappiness or worse is just around the corner. So how can you end the anxiety and the instability of constantly alternating between happiness and the threat of its loss and punishment?

Your peace and happiness come from the deep acceptance of your worth. Behind your perceived failure, disappointment or suffering there is often some degree of unworthiness to receive the reality of Love that was guaranteed in your creation. Knowing this gives you a powerful focus for your spiritual growth.

In addition to staying aware of the role of deserving in the manifestation of what you desire, there are many other steps you can take to help you accelerate the impact of this heightened awareness.

One approach is to write down the reasons why you don't deserve. Why *don't* you deserve to be happy? Why don't you deserve to have everything you want? Many of us don't even realize we feel a primary sense of unworthiness, much less enumerate the reasons for this feeling. Not that you can identify all the specific reasons for the set point. Many of them are unconscious. But the very act of questioning why you don't deserve, helps you identify some of the reasons for your conclusions.

After you have made your list, throw it away, shred it or in some other way dispose of it as part of the past you no longer want.

Your complete acceptance of your worth is the eternal, unwavering purpose of your Inner Champion. Again, this is the effect of its use of forgiveness. It looks completely past your beliefs in your lack of deserving, whatever their origin, and in that process restores the truth of your perfection. Again, the Forgiveness Meditation is a powerful tool for healing old memories that created the beliefs and feelings of not deserving. It's available as a free download from CDbaby.com.

Finally, sleep gives you a wonderful opportunity each night for profound help from the inner self to heal these feelings and transform your past nightmares into the dreams of peace and safety.

Meditation

As you go to sleep tonight, simply ask the inner self to lift the burden of not deserving that you've carried for so long. Know that it is your right to have this burden lifted, and let the inner self bring you the happiness that is your birthright.

Day 25. Demanding Your Birthright: You Deserve to Be Loved

Knowing you are deserving is the key to ending the constant cycling between periods of happiness to the inevitable return of unhappiness and from mild disappointments to disastrous experiences.

I suggested that one way to release the feeling of not deserving is to ask the inner self to lift this burden while you sleep. The inner self will give you all the energy and guidance necessary to restore the knowledge that you deserve to be loved. However, you need to stay conscious in this process. Your negative ego is the embodiment of your historic beliefs that you don't deserve to be loved and be happy, and it will try to lure you back to your normal set point of unhappiness and struggle.

It's important to remember your true partnership is with the inner self, not your ego. You are on a path to self-love. Your complete acceptance of Love will return you to your true identity as that self. This requires both your compassion and your determination, because it is a complete reversal of the deadly weight of failure and punishment that is deeply woven into the fabric of your experience in this world.

For a while, even though you are more aware of your right to happiness, you will still experience frustration, anger, confusion and other feelings as you continue to grow and change. This is because old patterns will continue to interfere with your happiness. Simply acknowledge these feelings and release them. The ego wants you to deny these feelings of doubt and would have you believe they show your lack of spiritual growth and, of course, your lack of deserving.

Know that nothing could be further from the truth. The release of feelings your ego defines as negative is essential to remove the debris hiding your self-worth. Acknowledge and honor your feelings. They are important sources of information about your state of being. They should be accepted and not judged.

Resist the temptation to tell yourself that the events that frustrate you must be tolerated because you can't really expect continuous peace and happiness. Here too, you can sense the ego at work trying to get you to compromise and be willing to accept just a little bit of suffering, punishment or unhappiness. Notice how you react to hearing you have the right to peace and happiness or that anything that disturbs these states violates your rights. You may hear yourself say, "That can't be true!"

Let yourself feel this too, but realize, again, the inner self knows your loving heritage and it is very different from what you've learned. The inner self knows that only love is real, and in its limitlessness gives without compromise.

Spiritual growth honors our natural defiance. This is the angelic loving nature we all share that rebels against what mankind believes in: its limitations, its illnesses, its excuses. You might think of your transformation as the service of demonstrating the truth of Love. This is a path of championship. It is a path that opens naturally when you're in a state of deserving.

As I began to integrate my emerging spiritual growth with my clinical work, I created my first meditation CD, *The Land of Love*. Although it was initially used to help young children who were traumatized by violence, it has since been used by people of all ages as a powerful aid for sleep and healing. In the meditation, the inner self is personified as Alayah, the Fairy Godmother, who takes the listener on a journey to the Land of Love for a delightful and transforming experience. One of the gifts the listener receives is a beautiful purple shield for courage. This is a powerful healing image you may use as well.

Meditation

As you start this day, close your eyes and take a few relaxing breathes. See your inner self give you this shield. Sense all of your self-doubt being released as you accept the power of Love. Open your eyes and feel its presence throughout the day, reminding you of the courage and the championship of a spiritual path that springs from your deserving.

Day 26. Exchanging the Self You Made for Your Real Self

Each of us has a set point for happiness based on our perceived sense of deserving. If our experience of happiness exceeds this point, there'll be an automatic adjustment downward producing the disappointment or circumstances needed to lower our happiness to predetermined levels.

This set point is not a vague quality that has limited significance in one's life. It's a very specific calculation that comes from decades of evaluations about our deserving, based on our early experiences.

It is the inevitable product of our striving for love and affirmation from others, fueled by the deep knowledge of our worth that comes from the Love we share in our oneness with the inner self. When we are born on the physical plane, we step away from this knowledge and immediately seek this Love in the world.

But the certainty of Love we knew in our spiritual home quickly fades as we become intent on developing a self that's pleasing to others, a self that will bring the approval we so desperately need. We look for confirmation of our worth outside of ourselves and begin to accept others' opinions of us as valid reflections of who we are.

Our profound knowledge of the reality of Love, both as a limitless gift and the essence of our identity, is quickly lost as we shape our personalities according to our need for love and approval from others.

Love becomes conditional. It's based on our perception of deserving determined by everyone and everything around us. Thus, the self that we come to accept as real is built on a foundation that has nothing to do with the identity we share with all living things in the reality of Love.

There is beautiful statement in *A Course in Miracles* that says, "If you could accept the world as meaningless and let the truth be written upon it for you, it would make you indescribably happy."

Meditation

Begin tonight to joyfully take this wisdom with you into your dreams. As you close your eyes to sleep, see a picture of yourself standing before your loving, inner self. Imagine a zipper from your throat to your pelvis. See yourself unzip it to reveal a tablet that holds the identity you have written as your own. Reach in and give it to your inner self. Watch as it gently brushes away what you've written and inscribes the truth about you, gently replacing it within you. Then ask the inner self to fill your dreams with the happiness that only the truth can bring to you.

Day 27. The Vow of Your Inner Self to Bring You Home

Everything we have ever wanted - for ourselves, for those we love, and for our world - already exists in the reality of our relationship with the inner self. In fact, *more* than everything we have consciously hoped for is waiting to be claimed because we truly cannot even imagine, from the limited perspective of the personality, the joyous reality within us.

We can experience this reality at any time, especially in our dreams when we turn away from the intense focus on our physical selves, and step back into the spiritual realm.

Consider this for a moment. We were created from the exuberant, inexhaustible desire of Love to *extend its Love* through us as its creation. As I suggested earlier, the Declaration of Independence asserts powerfully and beautifully the vow inherent in our creation, that we are endowed by our Creator with certain unalienable human rights, and among these are Life, Liberty and the pursuit of Happiness.

This language expresses the deep knowledge of a loving Creator that inspired our forefathers. That same knowledge is within each of us and we can never be separated from it. This is the vow of Love. Our identity as the child of a loving Creator, with all the attributes and the wonder of this parentage has not changed because *we* perceive our errors and disasters to be real and unchangeable.

Our inner self continues to be perfectly undisturbed by the decision of a tiny aspect of itself to have a momentary adventure as a physical construct. But our powerful connection to its Love is also continuous. The inner self vowed to bring us back to the awareness that we are one and we agreed to be faithful to our heritage. Even though we wanted to experience the limitations of human nature to learn more about our freedom and ourselves, we expected to consciously return to our true self after our innocent experiment in the world.

To your negative ego, of course, this is absolute nonsense! It will try to convince you that you are nothing but flesh and bones, sinful and undeserving. It will try to persuade you that only through what it teaches you about the manipulation and domination of other people and things will you have a chance for meaning of some kind, but never happiness. And it will lead you on, endlessly looking for meaning where it cannot be found because this isn't your home. *A Course in Miracles* describes this as the 'song of the ego,' which is 'to seek and do not find.'

This is why dreams offer such amazing opportunity each night. They're a bridge to your reality in Love, and they are meant to bring you the happiness that awaits your remembrance of it.

The dreams the inner self holds for you will bring you home again by degrees. That is, as you're willing to exchange the dream you're separate from the inner self, for the certainty of your oneness, you'll awaken each morning carrying more of what is real into your days.

Meditation

When you close your eyes to sleep, see yourself encased in the armor of your physical beliefs. See the entrance to your dreams in front of you, with the inner self waiting for you. Then forcefully throw off your armor and step through the entrance. The inner self will take your head in its hands, pressing Its forehead against yours, giving you back your lost dreams of hope and happiness. Savor this moment. Then take a few gentle breaths and let yourself sleep in peace.

As you make room in this way each night for the transfer of your reality into your conscious experience, be sure to notice during the day experiences that surprise you with their miraculous quality. Because of your allowance, you'll find the inner self helping you bring more of what is real into your daily experience.

Day 28. The Healing You Long for Has Already Occurred

When your belief structure is finally cleansed of all the debris from the past, it will be an immaculate frame for the flow of energy and grace from your inner self into your life and your world.

As you clear away the beliefs that created the limited self, you may be amazed to find that you really want to join with and become the vision of your inner self. But from the perspective of the little, physical self, it can seem like such an impossible task!

How can you really know that it is possible to become this self? As you open your heart and let yourself desire and truly feel the reality of the inner self and its love for you, you *can* know this beyond any doubt. You can know that not only is it possible, it has already been accomplished. You already *are* this self.

This is easier to understand when you remember that it was a tiny aspect of your inner self that innocently wanted to become physical. In order to know yourself, you wanted to see what it would be like to be separate from your inner self and experience chaos, limitation and fear rather than the reality of peace, safety, freedom and love.

This was a completely innocent desire. But this little step away from the magnificence of your spiritual home was instantly terrifying, as your playful experiment became a nightmare that you thought was real.

Now imagine for a moment the response of the inner self, who loves you limitlessly. In the same instant you made this error and were terrified the inner self out, of its boundless love for you, healed your misperception and returned you to the full awareness of your identity as the magnificent self that you are.

In a sense, your deep desire to correct your original error has prevented the realization that it was healed long ago. You have become so seduced by the desire to heal the nightmare you believe you created, and so convinced of your unworthiness because of it, you decided you don't deserve to be healed and therefore have not realized it has already been accomplished for you.

The reality of Love and its healing is eternal and unaltered by your refusal to acknowledge it. It is still present and offered to you again and again in each instant. You need to finally become willing to accept it.

Meditation

Here's a meditation to help you feel the love that can take you back to the awareness that you already are this great self and have never been anything but this self.

I recommend that you use music you love with this meditation. Then close your eyes and picture someone you deeply and completely love. See your beloved suffering in some way. Open your heart and feel yourself instantly roused to action, focusing your love like a laser beam to restore this one to peace and safety.

Now open your *own* heart infinitely wide to receive the limitless Love of the inner self in response to *your* suffering. Breathe in this Love for a few moments and then open your eyes.

Know that we cannot hold the inner self to a lower standard of Love than the one we hold for ourselves.

WEEK FIVE -
TAKING BACK YOUR TRUE IDENTITY

Day 29. Consciously Choosing Your Present Innocence

As you imagine your own heart-felt desire to instantly end the suffering of someone you love, you start to realize that the infinite Love of the inner self could do no less.

When we stepped away from our spiritual home to experience ourselves in the physical world, we did this for a completely innocent purpose. But that step proved terrifying. What was supposed to be a playful experiment caused a devastating belief that we were alone, without Love.

In our frantic desire to fix the horror of that first step away from our home, we made endless attempts to return to Love, by struggling to heal all the failure we believed we had created. When you can understand that the inner self, as our Champion, instantly corrected that first mistake, you can use this awareness to motivate and discipline yourself each day to accept this healing as a source of power in your life.

In the deepest sense, living in the present moment does not mean using your physical eyes to pay better attention to what's going on around you. It means that each day you can choose to remember the power that is available to you because you are already healed. Your vision does not have to be blurred by the past. When you start feeling anxious about some perceived problem, you can practice shifting your focus to the alignment with the Inner Champion that is already present for you.

Within the purity of your true self, everything is possible for you. The solutions to complex problems, the peace, the courage and the miracles are all there for you already. They are probable versions of your experience, ready to be drawn into your life from your state of complete innocence and deserving.

Remember that this self is who you are. You don't have to go looking for It. It's a vibrant, magnificent energy within you. It should be the very first resource you turn to when you're faced with a problem.

Meditation

When you find your peace disturbed in some way, or sense yourself becoming mired in a complex situation, practice closing your eyes for a moment and consciously imagine yourself pulling a shade down over the situation. Then feel yourself step back into the healing light the inner self has already given you. Take a few breaths and immerse yourself in this supportive energy.

Then open your eyes and carry your worth and gratitude forward into the day. See what solutions come from your willingness to shift your focus in this way

Day 30. Opening Yourself to the Guidance of the Inner Self

You already *are* the magnificent, true self you so deeply want to be. This is the self you are when you peel away all the illusions you have accepted about yourself in place of Who you truly are. You will see everything you want for your life and your world more and more as you accept your inner self as your real identity. You will be more relaxed and confident as you learn to step aside and let your inner self demonstrate its grace and power through your physical self and into your life.

My friend, Tim Gallwey, the author of *The Inner Game of Tennis* and many other books on this subject gave ABC a famous and brilliant demonstration of the power of the inner self to respond to our needs when we get out of its way.

When his book came out, he was approached by Harry Reasoner to prove his claim that anyone could play tennis, regardless of their aptitude, when they were coached to let the natural abilities of the inner self, which he calls Self 2, come through without their interference.

In less than twenty minutes, he taught a woman in her fifties, who hadn't exercised in twenty years and had never held a tennis racquet, how to play tennis. He gave her simple instructions that distracted her from her personality's effort to learn the game. This allowed the inner self to show her the effortless performance available for her as she let *it* play without her conscious attention to *learn how to* play.

You may want to watch the demonstration yourself by googling '*The Inner Game of Tennis* on ABC.' It's an astonishing display of the energy that flows through each of us as we're willing to be a pure vehicle for the grace of our inner self.

All of our experience is created for us in exactly this way. We're either allowing the inner self to show us its effortless response to what we want or we are interfering with its brilliance by trying to create our *own* answers. Let the inner self coach *you*.

Meditation

Close your eyes gently and let yourself relax. Feel yourself standing alone in a heavy, dark cloud. Briefly imagine the weighty problems you expect to encounter today: the people, the situations and the worries that plague you. Now see the inner self surrounded by Light, seemingly far in the distance. Let yourself feel joyous as you speed easily through the darkness with the Light growing brighter with each step. Then burst into that brilliance, into the arms of the inner self and see your day sparkling before you. Open your eyes and resolve to bring this Light into your day.

Day 31. How Emotional Attachments Block Creative Ease

I suggested that you watch the ABC footage of my friend Tim Gallwey teaching an older woman to play tennis. By blocking her personality's effort to learn the game, her inner self came through and played the game for her.

All of our experience is produced in exactly this way. The inexhaustible energy of the inner self flows through us, creating our physical experience according our desires, our imagination and our expectations.

For example, the slightest motion of the physical body occurs because of our unquestioned freedom to move about. This movement happens effortlessly and involves the orchestration of millions of activities at the cellular level under the direction of the inner self. All of this happens according to our intent and the unquestioned expectation of our freedom in this regard, but without any conscious understanding of *how* it happens.

From the most minute action to the manifestation of your highest vision of yourself and your dreams, there are no limits to the power of inner self to fulfill your desires and bring you whatever you need for your greatest happiness.

However, when you want something that you are deeply, emotionally attached to, it's often more difficult to manifest the desire. But it's not because your inner self doesn't have the power to bring you what you want. Your emotional attachment to the outcome gives it a greater sense of reality or weight that seems to make it too difficult to create.

Even though in prayer or meditation you are asking the inner self to create what you desire, your expectation that it will occur for you and therefore the full power for its manifestation is weakened by your emotional attachment to the outcome.

The anxiety, fear and other feelings you have about the situation block the effortless creation you've experienced in other circumstances where you didn't have this emotional entanglement and doubt about the inner self bringing you what you needed.

Love's power is limitless. And knowing this is truly one of our greatest spiritual challenges. What seems miraculous to us is simply the expression of Love on our behalf, extending itself into our physical reality. Its limitlessness is our peace.

Meditation

The following meditation can help you deepen your assurance of Love's power and its peace. Relax for a moment and say to your inner self, "Free me from all the questions, doubts and fears that rob me of your gift of peace. Give me the serenity of knowing there is nothing that your mercy and Love for me cannot change."

Day 32. Manifesting Wealth: Your Right to Prosperity

We may often think of the inner self the way we think of our dreams. It doesn't seem real to us at least not as real as the physical self. However, the inner self, our true self, knows *we* are the ones who are dreaming. Our reality as spiritual beings is eternal and we cannot change our identity. But we can and do dream we have become something else, and this is exactly what occurs in our physical experience.

The glorious, creative being that you are continues to enjoy the unbounded happiness and power of an unlimited state of Love and of peace. It continues its adventures, completely undisturbed by your struggles. In a sense, you might think of your inner self as a designated driver of this great energy that waits at the rear of this field of joyous action, patiently tapping its foot while it encourages you to let it bring you back home to your spiritual reality.

This is why, when we stub our toes in certain areas, the constant, compassionate guidance we're receiving from the inner self is "It's not real! Let me fix this for you and show you what *is* real!"

This is exactly what happens with certain areas of our lives or certain goals we've given more weight. Their importance to us creates an emotional attachment that gives them more 'reality' in our minds and interferes with the inner self's power to effortlessly deliver what we've asked for.

The physical body and money are two great examples of these common stumbling blocks. You may find yourself happily manifesting what you want in lots of areas. You can even point to some astonishing creations where you *know* the results come from your successful partnership with the inner self.

But in spite of these unmistakable successes, you may find that anything related to the physical body is more challenging. Whether it's a sore toe or an illness, you may expect it will be harder to have the change you need because of the greater weight most of us attach to the body. And here I'm *not* suggesting you refrain from seeing a doctor if you are ill. Use *all* the resources you feel are necessary to care for your health and your well-being. Then consciously allow your loving partnership with the inner self to *enhance* whatever interventions are used to improve your health.

Then there's money. We often automatically assume money is beyond our creative abilities. Even though we trust the inner self to deliver in other ways, when it comes to dollars and cents, we believe so deeply in the reality of money, and are so attached to its importance in our lives, that it seems beyond even the power of the inner self to manifest it!

Learning to release the weight we've given certain areas of our experience and see *everything* in our life open to the miraculous intervention of the inner self can be a challenge. It takes patience and practice.

The first step is to recognize that you *have* given greater weight or realness to a particular goal. Then if you're anxious or fearful, acknowledge your feelings and, rather than redoubling *your* efforts to find a solution, give the problem to the inner self.

Continue to acknowledge your heart-felt desire and let it go, turning your attention away from it to something else that's engaging for you. In this way you create the space for the inner self's solution to reveal itself you.

Here's one of my favorite stories about the manifestation of money. It meets all three of these conditions.

Several years ago my friend Jason got married and wanted to give his wife the home of her dreams. They found a beautiful old house they both fell in love with. They knew it would cost a great deal of money to restore it but were shocked as it soon became a true 'money pit.'

Months into the work Jason called to say he had just learned the rest of the reconstruction they most wanted would cost $565,000! He said he didn't have enough money to do it. Bitterly disappointed, he said they'd have to live without the changes they'd wanted to make in their new home. He was resigned to the loss, and said he'd focus on decorating the rest of the house instead.

One week later he got a call from a small natural gas company he had owned stock in for many years. He was expecting the call since he received a little dividend check from them each year. It had never been more than $15,000. The caller told him the company had gone public and asked if he were sitting down. The company was sending him a dividend check for $565,000!

Your Inner Champion can manifest whatever you desire, regardless of *your* perception of the difficulty it involves.

Here's a meditation you can use for additional power, when you when feel anxious about creating a heart-felt desire.

Meditation

Close your eyes. Breathe gently and slowly and let yourself begin to relax. See yourself standing on a platform against the night sky. The moon and the stars are shining and twinkling just for you. Look up and see your Inner Champion appear as a magnificent figure, filling the heavens with light and indescribable power. Then open your arms and let it rush into your physical form filling you with its limitless power. From your heart project this power as a beam of Light into whatever you strongly desire.

Then forget about it. Let the Inner Champion do its job, and you do yours. Relax and become a channel for grace in your life and in your world.

Day 33. Learning There Is No Price to Exact for Joy

Yesterday we looked at the importance of recognizing the weight we give certain goals or areas of our lives because of our emotional attachments to them. Our insistence that these areas are somehow more difficult to change interferes with the natural flow of energy from the inner self and its desire to manifest what we ask for.

As you learn to get out of the way and open *all* areas of your life to the loving energy of the inner self, you'll begin to see a corresponding expansion of the breadth and depth of your happiness.

You are supported and encouraged by the inner self in this process. As you realize you deserve so much more in your life, you are in effect reaching past your old set point for happiness. It's important to stay conscious as you push past that old set point and set a higher allowable upper limit for your happiness. Your new sense of deserving needs to become solid. This prevents your ego from tempting you to unconsciously allow some punishment for daring to stretch beyond your old boundaries.

You can stop a free fall here by first of all recognizing the probability this may happen and telling your negative ego very forcefully, "No!!! I've already learned this lesson! I refuse to pay a price for this happiness!! I am truly worthy of everything!"

Then let the energy of gratitude lift you safely beyond the old set point to a new level of happiness. Gratitude reverses many of the feelings that contribute to your belief in not deserving. You cannot feel self-pity, martyred or victimized when you're experiencing the empowering energy of gratitude.

Here is a beautiful meditation you can use to summon this great energy.

Meditation

Close your eyes and take a few deep, relaxing breaths. Now call forth your memory of a defining, deeply transforming experience in your life - one that filled you with tears of joy. You know exactly the experience to recall. Let yourself be immersed now in the joy of that moment. Let yourself feel a deep sense of gratitude for this experience. Then sense the inner self surrounding you with the peace and safety that gratitude brings to you, and know you are in the process of healing forever and ever. Rest with this for a few moments. Then open your eyes and carry this energy with you into your day.

Day 34. When You Become Discouraged About Your Growth

In spite of your confidence in your spiritual growth, there will be periods of time when you may become discouraged about your efforts to align yourself with the inner self. Something may have happened that was very disturbing to you, and you may suddenly question the validity of your transformation.

You may find yourself momentarily filled with self-doubt, questioning the reality of your inner self and the loving power you have begun to trust.

Depending on the seriousness of the problem and the degree of powerlessness you feel, you may find yourself angry with the inner self, believing it has abandoned you.

Even if you're not experiencing it at this time, this is a very common experience for anyone who has made a deep commitment to return to full awareness of his or her inner self. This is sometimes referred to as the 'dark night of the soul.' It is the despair and loss of self we may feel when we encounter the full force of feeling separate from the source of our own being.

Of course, the inner self can handle your anger very nicely. And in a sense, just as anger is meant to be felt and released in order to clear blockage at more peripheral levels of your experience, the release of fury toward the inner self when you believe it has abandoned you, is a powerful means of clearing the most important blockage you will ever face.

Without minimizing in any way the pain of this experience, know that when you encounter this stage of deep uncertainty, you are reaching that time in your own growth when you will release everything that distorts your true worth and keeps you from the awareness of your oneness with Love.

Your spiritual path is not something that was thrust upon you. It's the result of a sacred decision you made when you decided you had been away from your home long enough and were ready to return at last. And you need to trust that this is an essential part of your journey.

There is a wonderful ancient tradition often associated with this journey home. The inner self honors the physical self as a champion, who fights to return truth to his world. To prepare him for battle, the inner self gives him a sword and a shield. The following meditation honors this archetypal experience and will help you through this challenging passage.

Meditation

When you are ready to sleep, take this meditation into your dreams. See yourself kneeling before your inner self. Watch as this great Champion, holding a magnificent sword, gently touches your bowed head and then each shoulder. Helping you stand, the Inner Self will give you your sword and your shield, asking you to carry it with you wherever you go.

Then sleep with the knowledge that you will indeed carry them with you from this day forward.

Day 35. Self-Pity and the Refusal of Love

On your journey back to love, you may experience a personal crisis that seems to negate the love and happiness you were learning to trust. You may feel that your inner self has betrayed or abandoned you. You may have become prey to the negative ego's taunts, voicing your own fears, that you have been led down a false path and left high and dry once again.

Realize, however, that in spite of the temptation to feel you've been victimized in this process, this is a natural stage of the journey back to Love. It actually reflects your *own* decision to accelerate your spiritual growth by pushing you to a deeper trust in the reality of your relationship with the inner self and its power to create the best outcome for you in *any* situation. This is truly powerful. Whatever the nature of the darkness you're encountering, you have been vested with a sword and a shield for strength! You *do* have the vision to clearly see your choices.

You can let yourself be drawn back by your negative ego to the little self and immerse yourself in self-pity, stubbornly insisting that, given all the tragedy or chaos that self perceives, you can finally prove that love has abandoned you and your sorrow is justified.

But self-pity is the most toxic of all moods. Until you make a conscious decision to step out of it, self-pity will prevent you from accepting Love. When you choose self-pity you have arrogantly accepted the negative ego's assertion that you don't deserve to be loved, rather than the inner self's assurance of the immaculate self you were created to be and will remain forever.

Here's how this might look if your perspective were high enough to see what is happening here. All the heavens, all the angelic realms of light and the full infinite force of your inner self, all love you. Yet you, when you identify with the negative ego in this way, focus on an infinitesimally tiny speck you insist is real and unloved, feeling justified in your self-pity. And you are turning your back on the limitless Love that supports you.

Your other choice is to accept the reality of your sword and shield and the power of the love they reveal. You can accept that love and carry it back to your physical self and to your world.

Meditation

Here is a meditation to help you do this.

Close your eyes and take a few gentle, relaxing breaths. See yourself holding your sword and your shield. The inner self is standing behind you at the forefront of a magnificent vision of heavenly hosts sending you their love. Now lift your sword and pointing it to the earth project this love as a beam of light into your world, watching it explode in a joyous celebration of your gift of Love and liberty. Relax for a few moments, then open your eyes and carry this energy into your day.

WEEK SIX -
THE CHALLENGE OF CONSCIOUS CREATION

Day 36. Joining Forces with Time and Space

It is important to remember that your return to the inner self reverses everything your negative ego tells you is real. This includes both time and space.

Although we often feel we are at the mercy of time and space, they are actually meant to serve us by giving us the creative freedom we need to make the changes necessary for our personal fulfillment.

As quantum physics has demonstrated for decades, both time and space are illusions. They are different manifestations of energy that are fundamental assumptions about the nature of our human experience. Although in our ordinary awake state we experience time as a series of sequential moments and space as solid mass, both are fluid dimensions of consciousness. They are completely subject to change in the power of the present, unfettered by our limited, egotistical beliefs.

When you concentrate on your alliance with the inner self rather than the constricted beliefs of your negative ego, each present moment holds the potential for an infinite range of probable versions of experience. You can clearly see this in dreams, particularly in lucid dreams, when you are freed from the constraints of time and space and instantly experience the manifestation of your thoughts.

Instead of using these dimensions as the creative tools, we use time and space as weapons against ourselves, and what are supposed to be sources of liberation become a means to enslave us.

When we are anxious, we believe we are encountering something real, solid, and separate from ourselves, which we need time to change. But it is actually the frozen expectations we carry from our past that disturb us by camouflaging our true dominion in the present. This includes what may be our deepest fear that our return to the consciousness of our oneness with Love will take forever or may be blocked entirely because of our certainty we are unworthy of Love.

Take comfort in knowing that the limitlessness of Love guarantees your creative freedom. Because of this, you can choose to join forces with time and space and experience your freedom once again.

In the real present you are already healed and joyously experiencing what you perceive as your future self. Because both time and space are illusions, that future is available to you *now*. It is your right to experience your true, inner self *now*. As you accept this identity as the gift it is meant to be, the inner self will magnify its presence within you and radiate its light into your life and into a world that is sorely in need of your healing.

Meditation

Find your comfortable position and gently close your eyes. As you breathe softly and easily, let yourself see and feel a vision of your future self wonderfully happy, fulfilling your highest potential. Know that this version of yourself is already manifest and that your willingness to journey within will bring you closer each day to living this reality. Open your eyes and let this knowingness fill your day with hope.

Day 37. Lucid Dreaming and the Experience of Creativity

You have heard over and over again 'You create your own reality'. Most of us are dazzled and inspired by this idea as we consciously begin our spiritual journey back to the inner self. But how do you really know this is true? How can you become so certain it is true that you can really enjoy the freedom it is meant to bring you?

The inner self is constantly trying to show you that your experience flows from within you, as your consciousness descends through your desire, your imagination and your beliefs into physical form.

Lucid dreaming is a very dramatic way for the Inner Self to show you that you indeed create your own reality. In lucid dreams you are awake and fully conscious while you are still dreaming. Without the limitations of time and space, your thoughts are instantly manifested. These dreams are opportunities for the undeniable experience of your power, and can teach you much about your multidimensional nature, defying all ideas about the limitations you have deeply believed about who and what you are.

Because of their potential for teaching us so much about our real abilities, lucid dreaming is not only sought after by those on a spiritual path, but also by scientists who want to study this phenomenon.

I'm going to describe my own initial experience with lucid dreaming. I hope it will inspire you and give you greater confidence in your own creative freedom, and the value of dream exploration.

First, I tried for several weeks to have a lucid dream before I was finally successful. I went to bed each night telling the Inner Self to "Bring my waking consciousness into my dreams." And day after day I woke up with no recollection of having any dreams, lucid or otherwise.

Finally, one night, when I was really beginning to think I lacked the power to do it, I intensified my resolve to be successful.

And that night I woke up, literally, within the dream state. I knew I was dreaming and I was fully conscious. I felt a dramatically heightened sense of perception. My body and everything around me had a luminous quality, as if my perceptions were infused with a brilliance I had never known before.

In this state our feelings are heightened and we still carry our primary beliefs. At that time in my life, I was feeling deep remorse over the death of a child who was killed on my watch as a child protection supervisor. Because I was still immersed in guilt, my dream was initially frightening. In the midst of my fear, I felt a strong desire to change what was going on in the dream, and a remarkable thing happened. I not only heard very clearly, but also felt that I *became* the idea that suddenly filled my head: 'You create your own experience. You can alter it at any time.'

Each time I thought this, the environment immediately changed. By the final sequence of the dream, I had repeated experiences of being able to consciously and instantly change situations that were frightening into events that filled me with joy.

I felt exhausted and wanted the experience to end. Again I felt myself *become* the idea: 'You can change your experience at any time,' but this time I held on to it. At that moment I knew I was creating my experience, and I was the one who could change it.

I shouted excitedly, "I want to go home to my own bed!" Instantly I was in a room with a series of beds like mine, all made up invitingly. I dove into the most appealing, and turned over on my back. Immediately what seemed to be a wall of darkness appeared before me, and the foot of the bed lifted to plunge me headlong into this black void. My dream body vanished and, fully conscious now, I moved from the dream state into physical reality.

The transition between dimensions occurred with incredible speed and force. Because of the density of this dimension in contrast to the speed and light of the dream state, I experienced the movement into my physical body somewhat like running through a brick wall. At the instant of direct transition between dimensions, I felt a diffuse sensation of nausea as my dream body became what appeared to be millions of tiny particles that coalesced into my physical body, which slipped into my own bed.

To an observer, the process my dream body went through would have looked like a scene from "Star Trek" following the captain's oft-used command, "Beam me down, Scotty."

As I sat up, I was still reeling and feeling a bit nauseous. Was my body the same as when I went to sleep? It was. Then the magnitude of my experience struck me. "I've done it!" I thought, excitedly. "*That* was a lucid dream!"

Not only had I experienced a lucid dream that was clearly designed to show me my thoughts create my reality, but I was also given the unforgettable gift of proving this to myself in the physical world, by consciously experiencing the recreation of my physical body from its energetic cellular structure through to its full physical form.

I will talk more about the implications of this experience, as I discuss the responsibility we share for bringing the justice, the love, the peace and the safety of our spiritual heritage, from our dreams into this world.

Meditation

You can practice your own role in this transition by gently closing your eyes and letting yourself briefly relax. See yourself high above the earth in your true form as a champion. Then see this mighty self descend to earth into your physical form. Beam *yourself* down, translating the love that you truly are throughout your life and your world. Then open your eyes and expect to carry this energy with you, throughout your day.

Day 38. Metamorphosis: Your Transformation to a New Form

Lucid dreaming is a powerful opportunity to experience how our thoughts literally become our physical reality. As you awaken to your creative authority, it is natural to question your right to this power and your worthiness to use it. Even though we are endowed with this freedom because of the limitlessness of the Love that created us, we believe that struggle and limitation are part of being human. Our sense of victimization is so deeply ingrained in our experience that the idea of complete dominion in our personal reality can seem superhuman and beyond our tiny reach.

As your desire for freedom becomes stronger, you can expect your negative ego to taunt you with an array of punitive objections at your audacity to think you deserve such omnipotence. But these tirades come from the ego's panic that you are joining with the inner self, because your acceptance of your spiritual identity is the end of its tyranny.

You might think of the negative ego as the core of all the distortions about yourself you have accepted throughout your life in place of who and what you truly are. The process of spiritual growth means that you are casting off your old form as a slave to your environment and exchanging it for your new identity as a free being.

When you fully return to your inner self, the physical self will joyfully serve your true identity, and you will not need the negative ego and its old limited beliefs.

This is why the butterfly is so often used as a symbol of spiritual transformation. Its metamorphosis from a caterpillar is a perfect analogy for the change in substance that occurs for us as we complete our spiritual journey.

The caterpillar spends its life eating. Then it enters a pupa state and uses the nutrients it has ingested throughout its life for its transformation into a completely different form, that of a butterfly.

When we start the journey back to our inner self, we use the energy of our life experiences to trigger a similar transformation. In a sense we have learned all we needed to learn about limitation in the physical world, and as the memory of our freedom rises, it creates an intense desire for the conscious reunion with our inner self.

This reunion can only occur as the result of a true metamorphosis. With our decision to go home, we enter a state of healing similar to the pupa state. This means going through a complete change of substance to emerge as the self that we truly are. We are not going to be a better version of our old self. Just like the transformation of the caterpillar to the butterfly, we truly become a new being.

You can take great comfort in this process. Even though your negative ego will fight for its existence by demanding that you give up the powerful vision of yourself that is unfolding in your heart and in your dreams, you don't need to bow to its clamor.

Meditation

Tonight, as you go to sleep, leave the negative ego behind you. Tell the inner self to release all your old fearful dreams. Ask to share *its* dreams of Love, and let you experience the transformation that only Love can bring.

Day 39. Letting the Inner Self Restore Your Peace of Mind

Our conscious reunion with the inner self is not only completely natural, you might say it's the *only* natural thing we'll ever do. We were created by Love, and we are destined to share the inexhaustible power and freedom that Love guarantees.

This reunion is the end result of a metamorphosis that occurs for each of us when we become truly exhausted from decades of limitation, struggle and suffering and wake up to the realization that these experiences cannot possibly reflect the will of the Love that created us.

With an intense desire for freedom, we then turn inward and go through a powerful transformation, emerging, not as a better version of what we were, but as a new kind of being entirely. This being is your true self, aligned once again with the creative power you were born with, ready to stand shoulder to shoulder with the Love that created you, and endowed you with the freedom you always sensed must be yours.

The inner self is constantly leading you through this transformation by demonstrating its total support for your needs and desires. This guidance is meant to be practical and unmistakable, and you can facilitate its gifts by being aware of it and open to it.

When you feel separate from the inner self, this sense of opposition is projected into your physical experience. To the degree that you feel this separation, you will sense this polarity with everything around you.

As you turn inward, back to your true self, this new belief in your integration will be faithfully projected into your experience in the same way your belief in separation was materialized. You will start to feel this integration as a real presence within you, and you will sense it, not just with the manifestation of new goals, but also as an increasingly relaxed awareness. You might feel it as a kind of ongoing melting process where, as you learn to relinquish control, the inner self will show you its ease in removing obstacles you were certain would be difficult for you.

As you let yourself accept and relax into this support, you will be surprised at how quickly you can see the evidence of your willingness to let the inner self clear a path to manifest your desires.

You can accelerate this process by setting your intention to let the inner self show you the ease of allowing it to take charge of anything that disturbs you. Simply notice any time you feel anxious as you think about a person or a situation. It might be something happening in the present or it might be some event you're expecting. It may be something you think should be insignificant, or it might be something you believe is important. The degree of difficulty doesn't matter. If you're feeling separate from the support of your inner self, everything around you has the potential to disturb you.

Meditation

When you feel your peace of mind threatened in any way, close your eyes for a moment and tell yourself with deep assurance, 'No!' You are going to let your inner self reshape this situation. Then project a blue violet light from your heart and surround the picture of whatever has disturbed you with the changeless peace that is your birthright.

Day 40. Accepting the Power of Love

We have been focusing on the demonstration of practical power by the inner self. The segment on lucid dreaming and others have been designed to help you recognize the power inherent in our relationship with the inner self and the responsibility for healing that comes with it.

As your relationship with this self deepens, you may wonder more and more about the extent of the power it brings you. As you really consider the nature of this power, you may be surprised at the questions you begin to have about its potential for healing in your life and your world.

You may realize the inner self is not only inviting you to let it heal aspects of your experience that cause you pain, but it is also challenging you to recognize both your opportunity and your responsibility to extend your healing to those around you.

We all are being challenged to remember the dominion that is our birthright. However, the realization of our true personal power often brings a range of feelings, from fear and anger to tempered enthusiasm and many other reactions in between.

This realization rarely brings joyous, creative abandon. Instead, it can stall our desire for reunion with the inner self, because the negative ego may issue thunderous warnings that accepting our power will somehow destroy us.

We have let the negative ego tyrannize us into believing we are powerless and are therefore justified in using any means of manipulation, control and domination to insure our safety. Of course, the ego isn't really interested in protecting you; it only wants to protect itself. It is the embodiment of your experience of powerlessness in the physical world and it is aware that the rediscovery of your personal power will end *its* existence.

As you question the scope of your personal power and responsibility, you may ask yourself many 'how to' and 'why' questions, trying to refute your power and protesting that it cannot be real. The problem with trying to disprove the magnitude of your power with a rational argument is that true power has nothing to do with reason. It is a matter of Love. We were created by Love and nothing we do can alter the perfection of our creation. This includes our shared identity with the limitless power of Love.

Our human experience cannot prepare us for the reality of Love. It is a journey away from Love and the limitlessness that is its meaning. As you learn to accept the depth of Love that you are, you will stop the useless egotistical debate about personal power. In fact, you will stop asking 'why' and 'how to' questions altogether and simply *become* the energy of Love that is the source of all power.

Meditation

Admitting you don't know the answer creates the openness the inner self uses to bring the answer to you. Each night as you go to sleep, tell the inner self "I accept that I do not know the meaning of Love. Help me take my waking consciousness into my dreams and learn what Love is. I'm willing to receive it now and hold it in my heart forever.

Day 41. Reversing the Deeply Held Belief in Powerlessness

Our fears and distortions about power and our resistance to accepting it can come from many sources, including our personal histories with the misuse of power. Throughout our life these experiences are a natural result of feeling separate from the reality of Love.

Initially, we develop our personalities in response to believing we are alone in this world, separate from the Love we only dimly remember. The shock of coming into this world without the Love we knew, fills us with fear, and we immediately try to compensate for it by controlling the environment we find ourselves in.

Our belief that we are separate from Love is projected into our physical experience, and it results in our perception that we are separate from everything around us. The power of the oneness we knew with inner self is replaced by a deep belief in our powerlessness, and we feel the need to exert a stranglehold on our personal realities to defend ourselves against the opposition we believe is real.

Seeing our delusion, the inner self calls to us, urging us to stop turning our boundless energy against ourselves. It's somewhat like harnessing the massive power source within us to extinguish the ocean of light we're immersed in, plunging us into darkness and then wondering why we don't see the light. The polarity we've created needs to be reversed. We need to accept the power of Love as the source of liberation it is intended to be rather than using this great energy to enslave ourselves.

Instead of the freedom and happiness that is our spiritual birthright, our denial of Love reverses the energy that's meant for our peace and safety. We end up using it to create a life of bondage and fear that requires constant vigilance and control to keep us safe.

The strain of refusing love is enormous because it's the continuous denial of our very essence. It puts incredible pressure on our consciousness and our bodies because we're resisting our natural state of being. We strain to hold up a little world we've made from our illusions about the nature of reality, while our rue self enjoys the boundless freedom of the real world within us, made from the power of love.

But you can always change your mind. You can decide to shift your energy away from the denial of Love and instead use it to welcome Love into your being.

Meditation

As you start your day, close your eyes for a moment and sense the presence of your inner self behind you. Now open the soles of your feet and let fear and control drain from your physical self. Imagine the inner self opening the top of your head, pouring a golden liquid of pure Love into all that you are. Feel its warmth as it moves through your body. Then open your eyes and carry this love, confident and relaxed into your day.

Day 42. The Natural, Miraculous Force of Your Energy

How can you bring more miracles into your life? You will be amazed at the miracles that unfold before your very eyes as you're willing to accept the truth about who you are and realize that miracles are your birthright.

We learn very early in our lives that miracles are, well miraculous. They are unexpected positive events that are totally outside of our natural human experience or control. We often use them as a last resort. When all else fails, when we have exhausted ourselves, struggling to change a situation that confounds us, or in an emergency where we're facing a serious situation we believe we're powerless to alter, we tell ourselves in desperation, "I need a miracle to save me!"

Because we may believe they come from divine intervention, a power beyond our puny reach, we assume we have to beg or plead with the inner self to bring us miracles. We think they're outside of our natural abilities.

But in truth, our nature *is* divine, and because we don't honor our own identity, we refuse to accept the natural miraculous force of our own energy.

The inner self is the core self that we are when we without our physical experience. Our inner self is powerful beyond anything we can possibly imagine. It is a force fueled by limitless Love, and it is charged with the responsibility to deliver the miracles we want and fulfill its function to bring us only happiness. Seen in this light, we can begin to understand what miracles really are. They are the release of the natural energy within us that is intended for our happiness. They appear when we give up the illusions that block their appearance.

This is why we often see miracles in life-threatening situations. It's not because the inner self taunts us by waiting until we are at death's door to save us, but because these situations can produce the rise and expression of powerful emotions that we've denied for a long time. When we release these feelings, we can create the space the inner self needs to bring us a miracle. And in these urgent situations, miracles often come with incredible speed. Almost like pulling back on a slingshot, there is so much latent readiness to bring us miracles, the instant we truly make room for them, the inner self joyously releases the force of its Love into our world and brings us the miracle we want.

To bring more miracles into your life, know they are the natural result of the creative force of Love within you. They are your birthright. By honoring your nature in this way, you cooperate with the desire of your inner self to bring them to you, rather than hindering them by asking for miracles and then fearing they won't come. Expect them to come easily for you. Your expectation is a powerful and necessary element in their effortless appearance in your life.

Meditation

As you gently close your eyes, let yourself breathe deeply and begin to relax. Feel the Loving energy of your inner self tickling the bottom of your feet and feel it move up through your legs, through the pelvic region and then up into your abdominal area. Sense it as an exquisite golden-white Light radiating in this, your core. Watch as it continues up through your torso, down your arms and up and out through the top of your head. Open your eyes and allow this Loving vitality to energize you and bring more miracles into your life.

WEEK SEVEN - FULFILLING YOUR DREAMS for YOUR LIFE and YOUR WORLD

Day 43. Pausing to Invite and Expect Miraculous Answers

If we could lift our perspective up above our physical self and see behind the belief structure that forms our ordinary experience, we would realize that we are immersed in a field of spectacular loving energy. This is the constant support of the inner self, sustaining every moment of our existence and always looking for the opportunity to bring us the miracles that are meant to be the fabric of our lives.

I suggested that miracles often appear with great speed in emergencies, when it seems there are no answers and we create the necessary space for the inner self, as our Champion, to bring us a miraculous solution.

In effect what happens in these situations is that our own beliefs, which ordinarily prevent the flow of miracles into our lives, no longer impede the energy of the inner self, allowing miracles to come through more easily.

You can also see miracles when you are in an unfamiliar situation and feel a sudden desire for a loving experience but have no idea how to create it.

Here is one of my favorite examples of this kind of miracle from my own life.

I had given my meditation CD, *The Land of Love*, to a friend whose eighteen-month-old daughter, Emily, had been suddenly frightened and was unable to sleep at night because of her fears. The first night she listened to the meditation, she fell asleep easily and her fears seemed to vanish. Her mother continued to play the CD for her each night for several years. By the time she could talk, she knew the story by heart and she spoke happily about the Fairy Godmother in the story, Alayah, calling her '*Princess* Alayah.'

When Emily was turning four, my friend Elizabeth planned a special birthday party for her. She asked if I would be willing to dress up as 'Princess Alayah' and surprise her daughter with a visit at her party! I agreed and quickly found just the right costume, complete with a crown and a magic wand.

When the time for the party arrived, I remember feeling anxious as I was about to knock on the door and make my appearance. I suddenly panicked, reasoning that I lived across the street from this child and saw her often. I wondered why I ever thought I could disguise myself this way and make her believe I was really the princess she loved! Impossible, I thought, but it was too late to back out. I swallowed my fears and opened the door.

The living room was filled with children, but I only saw the look on Emily's face when I came into the house. She was clearly transfixed and whispered excitedly, 'Princess Alayah, you *came!*' I scooped her up in my arms and sat her happily on my lap.

As she looked up at me, still wide-eyed and blinking in amazement, I put on the necklace I'd brought for her and secured the clasp. It was little gold chain with a tiny Star of David. Since she was still gazing up at me, I didn't think she really noticed the gift. Her little friends were all seated at my feet and were watching expectantly. So I decided to do a brief meditation with them and as I started, I remember thinking 'Please bring a wonderful gift with this exercise!' And before I could really count down and relax them in the usual way, they were all resting peacefully, like little rag dolls scattered in a playroom.

I left shortly after the meditation, hoping I could leave as if I were vanishing in thin air rather than just walking out the front door!

Elizabeth called the next day to thank me and tell me she was astonished at what happened. When I asked what she meant, she told me first that Emily really believed I was Princess Alayah! (In fact several days later when I came over for dinner, she was very excited as she told me I had missed seeing the Princess at her party!) Then she said Emily was still wearing the necklace I'd given her. When I asked why that was unusual, Elizabeth told me that Emily had never been able to wear any jewelry because of a severe allergy to metal of any kind! I hadn't known about this, but her mother told me it had always made the child sad, as both her mother and older sister loved to dress up and wear lots of jewelry!

To this day, Emily continues to happily wear jewelry and is still completely healed of her allergy.

This is a good example of what can happen when we are in a situation so outside of our normal experience. We create the space that's necessary for the delivery of a miracle because *we* have no answers. In this instance, my inner self could come through and give this child and me a beautiful and enduring miracle.

Meditation

Gently close your eyes and feel yourself begin to relax. See a situation you are struggling with right now. Picture your efforts to improve it. Then feel yourself relax more deeply as you listen to the inner self tell you, "Don't know the answer. Don't think of it, don't imagine it and stop trying to figure it out for yourself. Put it completely into my hands. See what miracles this brings!" Then open your eyes and begin a new, more miraculous day.

Day 44. Forgiveness and the Inevitability of Miracles

Miracles are the natural result of forgiveness. But it's not the forgiveness we learned as children. That concept of forgiveness is based on our belief sin is real. From the negative ego's point of view, we not only are capable of sin, our very nature is sinful. We may try to forgive others, and ourselves but the reality of sin dooms us to an indelible stain that defies healing.

Our unexamined conviction of sin's reality prevents us from responding to the loving voice within us that tells us we are meant to be happy. Intuitively we know that forgiveness is essential to our happiness and freedom. But in the physical world, because of our belief in the reality of sin, our attempts to forgive actually reinforce its reality in our consciousness, making true absolution both impossible and meaningless.

One of the most profound contributions of *A Course in Miracles* to our understanding of spirituality is its distinction of sin versus error. It teaches that although we can make mistakes, and believe deeply in our unworthiness because of them, these experiences are merely part of our dream of stepping away from our true self. Therefore, they cannot be real.

The inner self knows this. It knows that in spite of the fear and guilt the physical self experiences, it *cannot* sin. If sin were possible, it would mean that the physical self actually had the power to separate from its source and create another valid identity, transforming its immaculate spiritual nature into a sinful self.

True forgiveness is the function of the inner self. It uses forgiveness to heal the belief structure within us containing the memory of our errors and the distorted self-image they produced. When this structure is cleansed of those errors, the innocence of our original creation will be all that remains.

With this healing, the immaculate image you then carry into your physical life will be the same as that of your inner self. As its energy descends through you to manufacture your experience, the distorted beliefs of the negative ego that once blocked its

Love will be gone. There won't be anything left to stop the incredible force of what you are. Forgiveness has opened the floodgates of miracles in your reality.

The power of forgiveness lies in its utter simplicity, as the inner self replaces your perception of a sinful self with the purity of your true self. However, this simplicity is incomprehensible to your ego, so today I suggest that you begin the following exercise by acknowledging the ego's resistance.

Meditation

As you begin the day, close your eyes and say with confidence, 'Even though I cannot understand the simplicity and the power of forgiveness, I accept that miracles are the natural result of forgiveness.' Then see yourself surrounded by a brilliant emerald green Light. Relax into this beautiful, shimmering light and let yourself feel the happiness that comes to you as you accept the energy of forgiveness. Then let the inner self show you a picture of your life lit by the miracles forgiveness brings. Open your eyes and carry this Light into your day.

Day 45. Peace and Safety: The Guarantee of Love

Forgiveness not only opens the door for miracles in your life, it also restores the freedom Love guarantees you. When we come into the world, we leave the memory of our oneness with the inner self and the freedom of our spiritual reality in order to experience the inconceivable limitation of a physical self. We chose this, not as a punishment, but out of our exuberant desire to know ourselves more completely.

When we answer the sacred call of our inner self and begin our journey home, we will be guided more and more to see the evidence of our power. This guidance returns us to the inner realization of our freedom and the joyous responsibility that it conveys.

In this process of rediscovery, we will develop greater faith in our creative authority, testing the impact of our strongly expressed, new desires on our experience. The emergence of more miracles in our lives is a wonderful part of this process. Our willingness to accept forgiveness accelerates the delivery of the miracles we so richly deserve as the Inner Champion clears away the unworthiness that keeps us from receiving Love.

However, because we have lived with limitations for so long, we may keep our expectations limited as well. We may not notice those situations in our lives that are clearly meant to help us see our bondage to the past and recognize that our right to freedom is still being violated.

It is important to tell yourself the truth about those areas in your life that frustrate you. For example, the pain in certain relationships that seem to defy healing, financial limitations, professional dilemmas or physical problems are all common arenas where we believe we're hostage to barriers we accept as real and cannot change.

We were given complete freedom of being in our creation, without exceptions of any kind. How could we have been given freedom that is real but has limitations? Peace and safety would be impossible. We could never be confident about our power to change the circumstances that disturb us.

Behind all experiences of limitation there is some touch of unworthiness that remains in our belief structure. You don't need to search for it, but you do need to accept the Inner Champion's desire to cleanse it for you through the power of forgiveness.

Meditation

As you close your eyes and find your comfortable position, see yourself in your favorite place in nature. Sense the presence of your Inner Champion standing before you, offering you a most beautiful blue violet robe. Know that it is only your perceived guilt that keeps you from the grace and magic of your own being. Forgive yourself and allow yourself to be healed. Joyously wrap yourself in the robe. Open your eyes and sense the garment of Light you wear throughout your day.

Day 46. Extending Peace and Safety into Your World

Each of us holds the memory of peace and safety deeply within our own consciousness. We were created in this state of being, and we are destined to return to our awareness of it as our rightful home. It is the foundation for the happiness 'endowed by our Creator.' This *must* mean we are meant to experience peace and safety in *this* world. Now, as we consciously reconnect with our loving heritage, we realize that each of us has a unique role in helping to bring the reality of peace and safety into our world.

Yesterday I stressed the importance of being honest with yourself about those areas of your life that frustrate you and you seem unable to change, despite all your efforts. Although the ego insists that our struggles and suffering are part of being human, it's essential for us to understand that these experiences violate our right to peace and safety and need to be healed.

The same egotistical beliefs that cause chaos in our personal lives are reflected in the chaos we perceive in the world. Forgiveness, as the Inner Champion uses it, is meant to return us to the awareness of our oneness with the inner self and all creation. As we allow ourselves to be healed in this way, the recognition of this union will extend automatically into our community, our country and our world in a form most suitable for each of us and our unique roles in this unfathomable process.

Now your ego will probably shriek that this is outrageous. It will try to persuade you that it is pure arrogance to believe *you* contribute to world peace. However, we are endowed with the unalienable right to peace; and if this is truly divine law, there can be no exceptions to this endowment. Peace with certain limitations or allowable violations has no meaning.

And because our endowment of peace and safety is changeless, it exists now and is available to us now. We have never been separated from either the source of our own being or from our experience of peace. The perception of separation only comes in the nightmare of wandering away from our reality, a nightmare from which we are finally awakening.

We are responsible for our part in bringing the reality of peace and safety into this world. And because time and space are both conventions, they cannot block the fulfillment of our function. That is, just as we can access the past and use forgiveness to free ourselves from past pain, we can also access our future experiences. We can go to our future, completed self and begin to receive the wisdom and knowledge of that self now to help us fulfill our particular roles in recognizing the consciousness of peace and safety, and its manifestation in our world.

This is not a process we must learn to do, rather it is simply a state of being we can become willing to accept. It is the natural result of our reunion with the highest vision of ourselves in the physical world. As we *become* this vision, it becomes what we are.

Remember the wisdom available in what you would think of as your future self and access the knowledge of your unique role in exchanging chaos in all its forms for the reality of peace and safety.

Meditation

As you start your day, simply close your eyes and take a few relaxing breathes. Ask your Inner Champion to help guide you as you look up and see a shaft of golden white Light open several feet above your head. As it descends over you, it forms a cylinder. Stand within it and feel yourself being lifted to a soft cloud-like space. Sense as you reach this gentle space, that you are receiving the memory of all that you need to bring heaven once again to the earth you love. Let yourself drift down again. Open your eyes and relax knowing you will continue to be guided in this process. Step into this space and let yourself be lifted gently during the day any time you want to renew your experience.

Day 47. Experiencing the Peace of Your Future Self Now

The peace we are guaranteed is available to us now. Your inner self does not have to wait for us to grow up spiritually for us to be at peace. We are in that state of being now. We are simply not conscious of it because we are focused in a perception of time and space we identify as our present. However, because time and space are illusions, our consciousness has great freedom to access the wisdom and knowledge of what we believe is our future self and *its* experience of peace now.

Again, you might think of this future self as the completed or highest version of yourself in the physical world. This part of you has used your cumulative experiences in the physical world to finally accept your transformation into an immaculate vehicle for the expression Love.

You can experience the power of this integration now as you realize you cannot be held hostage by either your past or by future experiences that simply repeat the past. You can choose to align yourself now with the wisdom and Love of your future self.

You're already doing this when you face a situation and suddenly feel it's an outrageous violation of your rights in some way. You may instinctively rise up at this injustice, and unconsciously perhaps, use the force of Love within you to alter the experience.

The only obstacle to our sustained alignment with the inner self is the structure that contains our physical histories and the beliefs they produced. This structure distorts our true perception and results in a false self-image we accept as real in place of our who we are.

When we feel a sudden and intense desire for change, we often temporarily over ride or disable this structure, allowing the force of Love to come through us and produce what we want.

As I suggested earlier, shamans can shift probable versions of physical reality to produce whatever is needed at will because they have learned to consciously set aside their personal histories and choose the power of their inner self instead.

On your own path to completion, *you* can choose the power of your inner self by consciously choosing to step away from your personal beliefs and allowing that self to come through you when you want a miracle to transform a difficult situation.

You can do this easily, not by trying to blast your way through your belief structure, but by approaching your inner self with the humility of the present moment that releases the power of love.

Meditation

Close your eyes and place your hand over your heart. Take a few relaxing breathes and say to your inner self, "Dearest one, I come empty handed this time. I open myself to receiving the full force of your Love. Let it course through me now and bring the miracle I want." Then open your eyes and let your inner self show you its Love for you.

Day 48. Forgiveness and the End of Punishment

It is impossible to overestimate the beauty and power of true forgiveness. It is the golden door your inner self holds open, to show you the quick and easy entrance to your completion and your infinite home.

In order to go through this door, we have to release the idea of forgiveness most of us have accepted since childhood. That idea is based on the belief that sin is real, rather than simply a mistake within the nightmare of perceiving ourselves separate from the reality of Love.

Once we believe in sin, the conventional notion of forgiveness can never release us from the guilt and punishment we believe we deserve. We may go through the ritual of forgiveness, yet we are still left with the perception of an eternal stain that effectively bars us from accepting our right to love and happiness. This dooms us to a feeling we are not deserving and that punishment is inescapable.

This is incomprehensible to the inner self. It knows your innocence. It knows that nothing you ever do can alter the immaculate nature given to you in your creation.

However, it also knows that you deeply believe in your guilt. It knows that the feeling of not deserving has tyrannized you and it knows the punishments you have heaped upon yourself because of your perceived deficits.

Meditation

Today, let the inner self open the door to true forgiveness for you at last. As you close your eyes to sleep, resolve to let this self bring you a forgiving dream. See it standing beside the golden door of forgiveness, lifting its lamp to show you the way. Then let yourself feel a profound sense of relief as you hear it say, "It's over! The punishment's over..." And see yourself walk through the door of forgiveness, knowing you're in the process of healing forever and ever.

Day 49. Manifesting Your Birthright to Peace, Happiness and Miracles in Your Life and in Your World

It can take a great deal of persuasion for us to finally accept the Love within us and to appreciate that our physical experience is meant to be a gift of this Love.

Many of us are stubborn. We might say that, given what we've had to contend with in our lives, our stubbornness is justified. Suffering and struggle against seemingly unending limitations have been deeply ingrained in our experience and our hearts. We can become so accustomed to and comfortable with the constant slaying of dragons, we don't want to be told they are our own creations; and we mightily resist the invitation of our inner self to turn around and accept the Love that makes them vanish!

But we are being pressured now to pay attention to the guidance of the Inner Champion as it shows us evidence of our power, so that we can finally, consciously create peace in our lives and in our world.

Years ago I was given a remarkable opportunity to witness the nature of this power when what appeared to be a 'real' physical event surrendered easily to the force of a loving intention.

I was out sailing one afternoon on a beautiful lake in Minnesota, with my friend Jill and Andrew and his wife, Barbara. Andrew was retired from many years in the Public Health Service, and I had recently persuaded him to come out of retirement to provide consultation in a senior mental health program. I was very fond of this tall, stalwart man, whom I considered to be a great, sweet spirit and a wonderful doctor.

Andrew had been navigating, and as we pulled up to the dock, Jill and I climbed out of the boat. We stood watching him busily tying up to the slip while his wife ran up to the house to start dinner.

Then, without warning, he tripped and fell forward, face down in the boat. Horrified, and before I could even cry out, I saw what I now know was the most likely probable future for him because of this fall. Andrew had broken his hip and was in a nursing home, his great vitality ebbing away.

Simultaneously, I felt what I can only describe as a massive burst of warmth that seemed to come from both Jill and me, focused with laser-like intensity on that image of Andrew. In that instant, I watched in amazement as if a film clip were being reversed, and he returned to his previous standing position!

Jill and I must have been standing there staring at him with our mouths open in shock, because Andrew was looking at us, puzzled, asking us what was wrong!

All I could do was sputter, "Oh my God, Andrew, are you alright?" And to this, he simply said, "Well, of course!" and smiled broadly at us as he hummed and finished tying up the boat.

Now, it's important to understand that all of this occurred in a split second and Andrew was not conscious of what had 'happened.' The entire sequence was produced to show both Jill and me the nature of personal reality and the power of Love in the present moment to shift to other probable versions of experience when we are faced with events we want to change.

When Andrew fell, we witnessed an acceleration of time and space to show us the most probable result of this action. However, the power of our desire to stop this series of events was immediately honored, producing a reversal of both time and space back to the original moment - prior to the fall.

This was a graphic demonstration of what actually occurs constantly in our experience as our choices determine the manufacture of our personal realities. We are, in effect, moving in and out of probable versions of experience in each moment as Love moves in our direction to express our desires.

And there is an infinite range of probable versions of experience and limitless power to produce our desires. To the Inner Champion, there is *no difference* in the level of difficulty in reversing a broken life, a broken country or a broken planet. As we allow the process of forgiveness to be real, we create the pure space for whatever we desire, and peace will be created for us just as effortlessly.

Meditation

Gently close your eyes and let yourself relax. Imagine you are in a place of great beauty standing at the bottom of a magnificent staircase. See your Inner Champion at the top of the stairs opening its arms for you. See yourself unzip your physical body and step out of it, revealing the brilliant Light of your energy body. In this form, see yourself fly easily up the stairs and become One with your Inner Champion. Feel the power of this Oneness as you turn and bring your Light back down the stairs. See the beautiful red velvet curtain you stepped behind on the stage that began your journey. Watch it part again to let you step onto the stage of your new world. Open your eyes and bring this Light with you into your life.

About The Author

Kathleen Quinlan is a Licensed Clinical Social Worker who has been practicing in her field for more than thirty years. She graduated *Summa Cum Laude* from the University of Minnesota with a BA in English and a Master of Social Work. Her postgraduate experience with world-renowned psychiatrist, Milton H. Erickson MD and years of study in a variety of spiritual traditions, including *A Course in Miracles*, have helped her create a unique synergy of clinical and spiritual approaches to healing.

Kathleen developed and administered many clinical programs in both the public and private sectors including interventions for breast cancer, infertility, HIV/AIDS and veterans with PTSD. She uses guided imagery and meditation in her work and has produced four powerful CDs for deep relaxation and healing:

The Land of Love
https://www.amazon.com/Land-Love-Kathleen-L-C-S-W-Quinlan/dp/B000MMN9PO

La Tierra del Amor
https://www.amazon.com/Tierra-Amor-Kathleen-Quinlan-LCSW/dp/B00N45NF1Y

The Thirty Day Meditation Series
https://www.amazon.com/Thirty-Meditation-Kathleen-Quinlan-LCSW/dp/B00BZ13RUI

The Forgiveness Meditation
https://store.cdbaby.com/cd/kathleenquinlanlcsw12

CPSIA information can be obtained
at www.ICGtesting.com
Printed in the USA
LVHW020637020120
642213LV00016B/404/P